Instructor's Manual

Steps to Writing Well Tenth Edition

and

Steps to Writing Well

with Additional Readings Seventh Edition

Jean Wyrick *Professor Emerita, Colorado State University*
Colleen D. Schaeffer *California State University, Northridge*

THOMSON

WADSWORTH

Australia • Brazil • Canada • Mexico • Singapore • Spain • United Kingdom • United States

THOMSON
WADSWORTH

Instructor's Manual
Steps to Writing Well, Tenth Edition
and *Steps to Writing Well with Additional Readings*, Seventh Edition

Jean Wyrick/Colleen D. Schaeffer

Publisher: *Lyn Uhl*
Acquisitions Editor: *Aron Keesbury*
Development Editor: *Camille Adkins/Cheryl Forman*
Managing Marketing Manager: *Mandee Eckersley*
Marketing Communications Manager: *Stacey Purviance*
Content Project Manager: *Karen Stocz*

Senior Art Director: *Cate Rickard Barr*
Photo Manager: *Sheri Blaney*
Print Buyer: *Betsy Donaghey*
Cover Designer: *Gary Ragaglia*
Compositor: *GEX Publishing Services*
Printer: *West*

Cover Image: The Walk, 1890 (oil on canvas), Sisley, Alfred (1839-99)/Musee d'Art et d'Histoire, Palais Massena, Nice, France, Lauros/Giraudon/The Bridgeman Art Library International.

Printed in the United States of America
1 2 3 4 5 6 7 11 10 09 08 07

10-Digit ISBN 1-4130-3228-1
13-Digit ISBN 978-1-4130-3228-4

Thomson Higher Education
25 Thomson Place
Boston, MA 02210-1202
USA

For more information about our products, contact us at:
Thomson Learning Academic Resource Center
1-800-423-0563
For permission to use material from this text or product, submit a request online at **http://www.thomsonrights.com**
Any additional questions about permissions can be submitted by e-mail to **thomsonrights@thomson.com**

Contents

Overview of *Steps to Writing Well*

Part One—The Basics of the Short Essay provides fundamental instruction for college-level writing expectations, addressing all aspects of the writing process from prewriting through final draft, with discussion and practice sessions that employ strategies for drafting and revision. In addition, introductions to creative and critical thinking, effective sentence construction, word logic, and connections between reading and writing link students to essential details in the writing process while giving them the language to talk about writing. Equipped with these tools, students can begin to effectively negotiate the more detailed instruction and advice that Part Two—Purposes, Modes, and Strategies illustrates, while putting to use new skills and knowledge gained from Part One.

Part Two emphasizes strategies for developing ideas and text, organizing text, analyzing text, and assessing and revising text. The major focus in this section involves developing text based upon audience needs and purposes for writing. While this section covers four basic strategies—exposition, argumentation, description, and narration—Wyrick clarifies that most writing does not exist in "any one mode in a pure form."

Rather, most writing reflects a writer's primary goal or purpose, i.e., an argument or a story, but entails a combination of writing types/strategies throughout. Once students begin to recognize the structural elements of each type, they can begin to employ the elements logically at all stages of the writing process—prewriting (discovery of topics, theses, audiences, purposes, and content), drafting, and revision. Chapter 13 ends this section with a discussion of combining elements, analysis of an essay using multiple strategies, and as in all other chapters, practice and suggestions for writing.

Part Three—Special Assignments focuses on writing scenarios that students will encounter in college and beyond, familiarizing them more fully with 1) college-level writing and research methods, strategies, and formats, including using library and online sources; 2) practical advice on how to respond effectively to timed writing prompts, with special emphasis on the "Response" essay; 3) basic ways to read, analyze, and develop intelligent responses to literature and poetry; 4) additional perspectives on ways to assess and write about film and film reviews; 5) the do's and don'ts of business writing, covering such elements as memos, letters, e-mail, and résumés; and 6) an exciting new Chapter 17 that explains the specific and often overlooked ways to write about the visual arts of painting, sculpture, and photography. Not only will students have an opportunity to learn about how artists and their community value the visual arts, they will learn to apply this knowledge to the many new visuals within *Steps*. Likewise, instructors hoping to cover each of the major concerns in this section can easily develop units using the topics here as themes—text-response, research, literature, work—incorporating chapters from other sections as appropriate. For instance, Chapters 8 (The Reading-Writing Connection), 9 (Exposition), 23 (Development by Example), and 25 (Comparison/Contrast) could comprise a unit on text-response or timed writing. Add Chapters 16 and 33 (both of which focus on poems and short stories) and a unit on literature is born. Chapters 10 (Argumentation), 13 (Writing Essays Using Multiple Strategies), 26, 27, 28, and 29 will build a strong scaffold for both analyzing and creating arguments. Finally, teachers wanting to incorporate work themes into their classrooms can begin or end a term with Chapter 19, asking students to create real résumés.

This Instructor's Manual has additional suggestions that build on Wyrick's assignments in Chapter 19. Writing that allows students to see a goal beyond the classroom and a grade is writing that has a "real" purpose for students, and it can and does generate an enthusiasm in students that may be difficult to match in academia. As such, this chapter may be a good place for introducing students to the stages of full-length writing tasks. Chapters 1 through 8, which discuss process, can be incorporated into the discussion of considerations necessary for developing ideas about purposes, audiences, and organizing strategies in much the same way one would when considering what to include in a résumé—how to organize it effectively for different kinds of audiences, what to include in a letter of application, and in both cases, how to draft and revise using peer review. Effective use of sentences and words takes on a new importance when students realize that a teacher is not the intended audience.

Part Four—A Concise Handbook follows Chapter 19 and offers support for those students needing to sharpen their grammar skills and also helps the students who are newly concerned with the impression their writing might have on an audience.

Part Five—Additional Readings includes twelve chapters of added readings, emphasizing exposition, argumentation, description, narration, multiple strategies, literature, and writing and language. These chapters can be used in conjunction with Part Two reading assignments, either through themes suggested within the essays or through organizational considerations, as Wyrick's text seems to suggest. In addition, should instructors choose to create units based on suggestions here about Part Three—Special Assignments, the additional readings will provide a variety of examples for further in-depth analysis and discussion. At least one new essay or poem has been included in each chapter in this section. Wyrick has chosen challenging texts that offer not only clear examples of writing strategies and processes, but interesting, timely, and perhaps timeless topics for discussion.

■ Suggested Teaching Tools to Use with *Steps to Writing Well*

The composition maxim "The only way to learn to write is by writing and rewriting" is underscored in *Steps* as a premium is placed on writing and revision through creative and critical thinking (Chapter 5). Keeping journals (Chapter 1) and participating in collaborative activities (Chapter 5) are two ways instructors might encourage students to examine their own writing process and analyze the writing of others, enabling them to bring new insights to their own work.

■ The Journal

Chapter 1 of *Steps to Writing Well* discusses the benefits of keeping a journal and offers students suggested uses for the journal. Jean Wyrick notes that there are numerous advantages in requiring a journal:

Benefits for the student:

- encourages thinking, learning, discovery
- helps sequence the student's writing processes—provides practice of skills
- improves the quality of the written product—reduces writing anxiety
- improves class participation

Benefits for the teacher:

- provides opportunities to intervene in the students' composing stages
- ensures better "products" to evaluate
- may replace traditional assignments
- may reduce grading time and pressure
- discourages "passive" reading of assigned material
- allows the monitoring of class progress, understanding of material

For journals to be an effective part of a college composition course, expectations for journal assignments should be clearly communicated to the students. The journal provides them with a chance to write informally, perhaps experimenting with their writing and taking more risks than they would in a traditional, formal essay assignment. This is not to say, however, that journals are not to be taken seriously by student writers: if journals are to be a success, with assignments that are rewarding for the instructor as well as the students, there should be accountability. When students are thoroughly invested in their journals, a great deal of learning can take place, but if the journal is not incorporated into class discussion and reviewed periodically by the instructor, the journal's effectiveness is likely to be diminished. Here is a sample description of a journal from one composition teacher's course guide:

In much the same way that an artist uses a sketchbook to record ideas and preliminary sketches for larger works, your journal is a tool for you to document your ideas and progress in the writing field over the course of the semester. Assignments for the journal will be varied and will take place both in and out of class. A couple of notes: be sure to title and date each assignment, doing them in the order they are assigned. In addition to written assignments, class notes should also be recorded in the journal. In short, your journal should be a complete record of your preliminary writings for each essay. A suggestion: consider reserving the last few pages of your journal to record assignments for each class meeting.

Structure

Please organize your journal by unit, labeling the first section "Introduction." As we complete each unit and move on to the next, title each section according to the writing strategy currently being explored ("Narration," "Description," etc.).

Grading

Journals will be collected at the conclusion of each unit, often the last class before an essay is due, and will be returned the following class period. Each assignment will be noted as complete or incomplete, with credit given for each thoroughly completed assignment. At the end of the term, your journal grade will be determined as a percentage (number completed out of the number possible) and converted to a letter grade.

When giving take-home journal assignments, detailed instructions help guarantee completed, thorough journal entries. Here is a sample assignment:

Journal Assignment Three

For most of this course, we have been discussing the importance of writing clear, straightforward essays that communicate directly to the reader. These were characterized by unity, coherence, a clear, narrow focus, effective paragraph development, and creative introductions and conclusions.

For this journal assignment, choose a *cover story* from any *Time* or *Newsweek* magazine. Then do the following:

- Copy it on a copy machine and staple it to this assignment sheet. Make sure the entire article is included.
- Use a pen or pencil to mark up the essay (unmarked essays are not acceptable). Make note of things like transitional devices, thesis statements, interesting concrete language, paragraph development, etc. In other words, try to notice as many of the things we talked about in class as possible.
- In the margin or somewhere near each mark, identify what it is you are marking.
- On a separate sheet of paper, write four or five sentences evaluating the essay, making some comment about the audience for which the essay is intended, the transitional devices used, and in general how you would evaluate the overall quality of the writing, based, again, on the things we have been discussing in class.

■ Computer Activities

For those who have access to computers in a classroom setting, any number of the Practice sessions, Writing Assignments or activities listed in the text can be effectively translated into lessons that employ computer use.

1. Classroom discussion can take place online through Inter-Relay Chat (IRC), HyperNews forums, MOOs or MUDS (multiuser domains), or even e-mail if circumstances permit.

2. Prewriting, which asks students to explore ideas and to find connections, often suffers from the urge to edit. Ask students to practice free writing in class and/or at home or a computer lab while turning off the computer screen. Some will be discomfited by this activity as it prevents the flow of thought from being maintained in the normal fashion—writing, pausing to read what one has written, editing, etc.

   Instead, the writer is forced to simply put down whatever comes to mind, even if that means not finishing thoughts. Freewriting in this fashion can generate a good deal of brainstorming that may or may not appear as completed text, but that is the intent—to generate material that one can later formulate into comprehensible text for a reader.

   This activity is a wonderful tool for the writer who has trouble "getting started," but it needs to be practiced regularly for the writer to be able to overcome his or her discomfort. In addition, because it allows for mistakes to be made and readily excused, those writers struggling with typing and/or computer use will benefit from this activity as well. As writers become more comfortable with the keyboard, the connections between thought and the physical production of that thought will "warm up" through the practice. Too often, this sort of practice is neglected and for those who have little typing experience, writing in college can be a miserable physical torture.

3. Most word processing software includes some type of template for outlines. These templates can be utilized easily in both brainstorming and organization workshops suggested in Chapter 1—Prewriting. Meanwhile, presentation programs, such as PowerPoint, provide written guidelines for text development. Moreover, PowerPoint itself allows for creative presentation of student text, and is especially useful to introduce students to electronic and multimedia forums for oral reports. Web pages, home pages, and the like require a bit more computer knowledge than some students have, so presentation software is an easier way to incorporate the principles of reader/audience-centered text development. Moreover, incorporating presentations into class content enables students to recognize more readily the benefits of audience analysis as well as the connection between text and context.

4. If Internet access is available, the most obvious benefit for first-year students will be easy access to research materials. Moreover, research itself can be not just a unit of study, but an essential or core element in the class, included in each assignment in some fashion. Ready access to libraries provides students with immediate access to biographical and historical data that may assist them to understand obscure references in readings, to gather additional information about authors, places, times, etc. Meanwhile, learning to incorporate sources while working in Chapter 14 can be enhanced by continued practice in doing so and by instant access to online handbooks and style formats when other such texts are not available.

■ Collaborative Activities

In Chapter 5 of *Steps to Writing Well,* students are given advice on maximizing the effectiveness of revision workshops. There are also guidelines for the composition instructor to ensure successful collaborative activities. Jean Wyrick offers the following advice:

Suggestions for Organizing Collaborative Activities

Small-group work and peer revision workshops sometimes aren't as productive as we'd like them to be. Here are some suggestions for organizing collaborative activities that you might find useful.

1. Hand out a sample student paper the class session before the workshop. Ask students, at home, to write a brief summary and to make a note of the paper's major strengths and weaknesses. Ask them to bring this paper, their notes, and their own drafts to class.
2. Hand out written instructions for the workshop or write them on the board before class. At the top of the sheet/board include a statement of your (realistic, limited) goals for this activity.
3. Discuss your goals with the class. Talk about the value of giving and taking constructive criticism. (What kinds of comments are most helpful, which aren't, etc.?) Go over the instructions for the workshop *before* they move into pairs or groups.
4. Clearly state in writing an "accountability factor." Students must always know they are responsible for producing something that will be shared with the entire class at the end of the activity—a report, something to be written on the board, a reading of a revision, something.
5. State the time limit for this activity. (Tell them less time than you really can allow for this activity.) Fifteen to twenty minutes on one activity is probably tops. Always leave yourself maximum time to discuss the results of the activity. Whole-class discussion time should always be as long as (or longer than) the group time.
6. Always design the groups and match up students for pair work. Avoid matching buddies. Keep track of who is working with whom from week to week.
7. If you're doing small-group work, assign jobs: a recorder to keep notes, a timekeeper to move folks along, a reporter to present results, a facilitator to lead discussion, a "devil's advocate" to introduce a different point of view, and so on. Make each member of the group responsible for something.
8. Discuss the instructions for the workshop. If you're running a revision workshop, the instructions should be a limited number of clearly defined, specific tasks. Too many tasks addressing every aspect of the paper do not produce good results!
9. A note on the nature of the tasks: avoid simple yes/no questions (Is this paragraph adequately developed? "Yup"). It is frequently easier for students who are insecure about their ability to critique to offer advice after they have described what they see. Example: Underline the main thought of this paragraph. Number the specific examples (pieces of evidence, whatever) that support this idea. Would the paragraph profit from additional support? Why or why not? If yes, where?
10. Model the tasks on the sample student essay that you handed out last class. Modeling the responses shows students what you expect and also builds confidence in their ability to address these tasks and to critique a peer's paper.

11. Allow students to add at least one question to the list of tasks. They may do this as a class, or if they're in pairs, each student may add one individually. (As the semester progresses, the class should gradually take over the list of tasks.)

12. Circulate as they work. Move quietly from group to group. Listen, ask questions, but try not to assume leadership of the group. Note any common problems you might want to address at the end of the activity. Announce the time; give nearing-the-end warnings when appropriate ("Ten minutes left—you should have finished the first three tasks by this time").

13. Put the class back together as a whole and call for the results from some of the groups/pairs. Discuss the results and then demand that students apply wisdom gleaned from the activity to their own papers. Actual hands-on revision is best, but oral responses are good if you're short on time.

14. Always allow students to have the last word on the activity. Why was/wasn't it helpful? How could it be improved next time? These make good journal questions, especially if students want to complain about a partner who wasn't giving useful feedback.

15. When the papers are revised, let the peer-editor have a read before the papers come in. A quick read-and-pass is also fun—interesting, too, how the papers get better when students know many of their peers will be reading them.

16. Have many, many workshops on a paper, not just one huge one toward the end. Vary the kinds of questions/tasks: reader-based, criterion-based, descriptive, evaluative, and so on. Fit the workshops to the stage of the writing process—one on purpose and audience, one on organization and development, one on mechanics—whatever fits your purpose, your students, and the assignment.

17. After you've read through the papers, consider "publishing" some of the better efforts by duplicating them for the class, using an overhead projector, or by reading them aloud. You don't always have to reprint an entire essay—you can also present the class with a list of effective sentences, phrases, images, or even "A+" action verbs that were direct hits!

Here is a sample assignment sheet for a small-group activity focusing on the argumentative essay "Students, Take Note!" (Chapter 10):

"Students, Take Note!": A Group Perspective

Instructions: As a group, discuss and answer each of the following questions. Choose a recorder to jot down group decisions, a facilitator to lead your group's discussion, a time-keeper (you'll have 15 minutes for this activity), and a reporter to present your findings to the class.

1. Consider the author's thesis. What evidence does the author give to support his or her claim? Why is/isn't this evidence effective? Where is the author most convincing? Least convincing?

2. Does the author acknowledge/refute opposition to his or her claim? Why is/isn't this effective? What are some arguments against the author's claim that the essay does not acknowledge?

3. Are there any logical fallacies in the essay? If so, identify them.

4. What is your group's assessment of the overall effectiveness of the essay?

■ Suggestions for Effective Essay Assignments

As student writers, we all either heard about or experienced firsthand the horror of the instructor who assigned papers with a vague verbal statement of topic, length, and due date. The students in this case are left with a bewildering array of questions. How should the paper be developed? Is research required? How formal should the presentation be? These unanswered questions often lead to confusion and writer's block, resulting in a last-minute "shot in the dark" paper that does not accurately reflect the student's writing ability. In short, vague assignments often yield unsuccessful essays; thorough assignments encourage clear and effective student responses. To revise a well-known phrase, "As composition teachers sow, so shall they reap."

While classroom discussions, activities, and *Steps to Writing Well* will provide students with thorough guidelines for approaching a variety of writing strategies and styles, an effective essay assignment is vital to ensuring that student writers are able to transfer what they have learned in class and from the text to their own writing. Instructor's expectations for major essay assignments should be clearly established, preferably in a printed handout that students can refer to throughout their writing process.

Here is a sample assignment sheet for an argumentative essay requiring research:

Argumentative Essay Assignment

Argumentative skills are a part of everyday life: on a daily basis, each of us makes claims about issues large or small. Consider the argumentative elements of issues that you're concerned about. To make this assignment a meaningful and successful endeavor, choose a topic of narrow scope so you can successfully support your stance. Consider the following guideline for your selection: *avoid* global issues and claims that are supported more by emotion or faith than fact. The key to a successful argumentative essay is to *combine cold, hard facts with logic to form a convincing argument.*

Once you've selected a topic, examine the subject for a debatable claim. If the claim is arguable (is there an opposing side?) you have the focus for an argumentative essay. To clarify your purpose and goals for writing this essay, it is vital to define a specific audience.

Argumentative essays must be fully *supported* with a combination of personal perspective and research. This is a research paper: in addition to personal knowledge you must use the following support for your claim:

1. a minimum of 5 written sources to provide current, relevant support for your paper. Attach a photocopy of all sources to rough draft.
2. an interview with an authority on the subject

Essay Length: 4–7 pages, plus Works Cited page

Due Dates

Topic proposal presentation/review: Tues. 4/14 and Thurs. 4/16

Completed rough draft due for take-home peer review: Tues. 4/28

In-class workshop on rough draft: Thurs. 4/30

Final draft: Tues. 5/5

For particularly demanding assignments, a follow-up "suggestion" sheet, guiding writers away from pitfalls the instructor has often seen in student essays, is sometimes helpful as students work to select a topic.

Guidelines for Selecting a Successful Argumentative Essay Topic

1. Is the topic narrow enough to be successfully and convincingly developed in a 4–7-page essay? A very specific topic, well presented, is more effective than a broad (if seemingly more significant) topic that can't be developed fully.
2. Is there a legitimate opposition?
3. Can you refute the opposition's argument?
4. Can your position be argued and supported primarily with fact and logic rather than emotion, faith, or a morality-based stance?
5. Is it an issue you have experience with or have a vested interest in? To be convincing, your voice must be heard.

Topics to Avoid

1. Issues that have been argued into the ground for years (e.g., capital punishment or the drinking age) unless you have a new angle on an old topic.
2. Issues that you feel so passionately about that you can't argue your position logically (rather than emotionally) or acknowledge arguments of the opposition.

After students have selected a topic and have begun drafting, a detailed reminder of essay criteria can be a valuable resource. A criteria sheet like the following sample not only provides student writers with a self-assessment tool, it can also be used in peer workshops as a tool for reviewing the writing of others. Finally, the instructor can use this same sheet as a grading guideline.

Argumentative Essay Criteria Sheet

I. FOCUS

    Clearly stated? _____

    Appropriate for scope of essay? _____

    Established as arguable topic? _____

II. SUPPORT FOR CLAIM

    Each statement of opinion/assertion supported convincingly? _____

    A logical rather than emotional base for argument? _____

    Avoidance of logical fallacies? _____

    Convincing support of overall claim? _____

    Acknowledgment/refutation of opposition's claim? _____

III. USE OF SOURCES

Use of required research sources?   _____

Effective use of sources as support?   _____

Context/introduction of authority?   _____

IV. STRUCTURE

Logical, coherent structure?   _____

V. MLA CITATION FORMAT

Correct format for in-text citations?   _____

Sources acknowledged appropriately?   _____

Correct Works Cited format?   _____

VI. MECHANICS

Free of mechanical errors?   _____

VII. AUDIENCE

Strong sense of audience/purpose?   _____

VIII. OTHER CONSIDERATIONS

Appropriate title?   _____

Effective lead-in?   _____

Clear transitions?   _____

Meaningful conclusion?   _____

Overall maintenance of focus/coherence/unity and development?   _____

■ A Few Notes on Portfolio Grading

Many times an instructor looks at a student paper and thinks something like, "If Mary just had one more shot at this assignment, she'd have it," or "With some additional evidence, this would be a darned good argument!" How many times, after a week or more of rest from a project, has Mary been able to look at what she's written and then make similar comments about her own work?

Because of the typical structure of a composition class, however, teacher and student too often have to settle for what can be accomplished in a given time frame. To combat these somewhat arbitrary and frustrating limitations, instructors now sometimes turn to portfolio grading, or more appropriately, portfolio writing. In a portfolio class, students write and revise assignments continuously throughout the term and submit a final collection of their essays for a course grade. The obvious idea is that students can achieve better results with the benefit of time and perspective to help them revise. In this way, then, portfolio grading is one way to match class structure more closely to current *process* writing theory. Students can be evaluated on their cumulative efforts, on their overall assimilation of class concepts, and on their revising ability.

Portfolio writing can be integrated into class structure in a variety of ways. A student's grade might depend, for instance, on one final review of his or her portfolio with no grades given on any writing to that point. Comments on drafts might include general strengths and weaknesses or notes regarding specific mechanical issues you are working on in class, but no score is suggested. Students are encouraged by this system to focus more on their process than just on the outcome. Instead of meeting an artificial deadline established only by the syllabus and a teacher's need to space assignments efficiently throughout the term, students can try an unlimited number of drafts, different versions, or new approaches, until they are satisfied with the result.

Another option is to collect and review student portfolios periodically, giving a grade for progress and quality at each review. Some teachers use a midterm and a final portfolio, concentrating the grade to between 66–75 percent on the final collection to maintain the emphasis on revision. Others choose to review portfolios three times during the term, once for progress, once for a preliminary grade determination, and once for final analysis.

Still other instructors employ a configuration that combines traditional grading with the portfolio concept. You might, for example, collect essays and give grades as usual, making sure to make comments directed toward the student's pending revision. Then students can rework these graded essays throughout the term for inclusion in their final portfolio, which will be reviewed for a final cumulative grade and averaged with their other term grades, similar to a final exam.

Whatever method is employed, successful instructors mold the style of portfolio writing to their own strengths and teaching styles as well as to their particular situations. The teacher with 100 students per term, a martyr indeed, cannot possibly do traditional grading and then tack on an additional element of portfolio grading if he or she intends to maintain any level of sanity. On the other hand, a teacher with one composition class might want to try using a number of individual conferences throughout the term, one or two preliminary portfolio reviews, and a culminating final portfolio. Assess your techniques and teaching conditions carefully and honestly, then design a configuration appropriate to those constraints.

When introducing a portfolio system, keep the following potential pitfalls in mind.

1. *Avoid grading your own work.* Too often, through well-meaning comments and directions, a teacher can appropriate a student's paper. Looking at too many drafts and making too many detailed comments makes the student dependent and stifles independent critical thinking. The student is then writing to achieve the teacher's vision of the paper, not his or her own. If a final portfolio reflects the teacher's expertise rather than the student's, the system is not working well. Questions ("What experience can you share to support this point?") and reader response comments ("At this point, I wasn't sure how these two paragraphs related") can be the most helpful in guiding students and avoiding this problem.

2. *Avoid grading **another** student's work.* As in any composition classroom, the portfolio class offers many opportunities for a student to get inappropriate help from others. A certain amount of in-class writing, of individual conferencing, and of requiring and checking multiple drafts will help minimize this problem.

3. *Expect and learn to manage student grade anxiety.* Students may worry greatly if their final evaluation will be satisfactory when they are not receiving periodic grades. On the other hand, some students may have an inflated idea of the quality of their work if they do not receive some early evaluation. Providing some method of early progress/quality assessment will help them understand where they stand in relationship to your standards. Such a preliminary assessment can be anything from an informal conference ending in a joint teacher/student determination of a grade and suggestions for improvement (a grade which is not recorded since every item is subject to revision) to a formal teacher-generated score that counts toward the term grade.

4. *Avoid increasing your workload.* While portfolio grading is not a way to cut back those lengthy hours of reading student work, it need not add to your hours either. The important thing to remember is that when you are looking at multiple drafts, you need not make as many comments on each. Pointing out one paragraph that needs a topic sentence, for example, and suggesting others can benefit from the same revision, helps the student review essays independently; and such instruction may lead to improved learning since the student is not dependent on your comments. Highlighting one or two comma splices and suggesting the student look for other mistakes of this kind can have the same result. Also, since the student is going to go back and rework these papers, you need not comment on issues you have not yet addressed in class. You can concentrate on single issues on each draft, a practice that will make both your job and the student's job more targeted and effective, less fragmented and frustrating.

5. *Avoid procrastination.* Some students might be inclined to hand in less carefully done work on early drafts when they know only the final product "counts." If you allow this to happen, you are either doing the student's revision work by reading and commenting or wasting your efforts before he or she has really put enough thinking or writing into the project. To avoid this problem, many instructors give appropriate credit for early drafts, encouraging students to present their best work at each stage.

Teacher procrastination is another possibility. Although the temptation might be to wait to look at papers carefully until the end of the term, only spot-checking early drafts, the quality of the final portfolios will be directly related to early and continuous guidance. Lengthy review and comments on the final collection might be interesting to some students, but will not be particularly instructive and will keep you working until the last minute before grades are due. One of the best ways to assign a final grade to the portfolio is to schedule individual conferences (these can be done in 15–20 minutes) in which the student reviews the portfolio with you and, together, you assess improvements, remaining weaknesses, and overall quality of the pieces in the collection, taking time to point out particularly strong revisions you have noted in several of the essays.

Implemented thoughtfully and individually, portfolio writing/grading can be very rewarding. For students, it can be a step toward more intrinsic motivation and greater independence as writers. For the instructor, it is a way to reflect a more realistic notion of the way good writing *really* happens—through a continual process of revision—and the portfolio can provide a better opportunity to observe and acknowledge substantive change in students' skills and habits.

Part 1

The Basics
of the Short Essay

C h a p t e r
Prewriting
p. 3

■ Summary

Getting Started

- you have some valuable ideas to tell your reader
- you want to communicate those ideas to your reader

Selecting a Subject

- start early
- find your best space
- select something in which you currently have a strong interest
- narrow a large subject

Finding Your Essay's Purpose and Focus

- listing
- freewriting
- looping
- the boomerang

- clustering
- cubing
- interviewing
- the cross-examination
- sketching
- dramatizing the subject

After You've Found Your Focus
Practicing What You've Learned, p. 18

Discovering Your Audience

How to Identify Your Readers
- determine who the audience is for your assignment
- if a specific audience is designated, determine its reasons for reading
- determine what knowledge your audience has of your subject
- determine your audience's attitudes
- determine specific qualities your audience might have
  - Readers don't like to be bored.
  - They hate confusion and disorder.
  - They want to think and learn.
  - They want to see and feel what you see and feel.
  - They are turned off by pretentious, phony voices.

Practicing What You've Learned, p. 22

Assignment

Keeping a Journal
- confront your fears of writing, conquer the blank page
- improve your powers of observation
- save your brilliant ideas
- save other people's brilliant ideas
- be creative
- prepare for class
- record responses to class discussions
- focus on a problem
- practice audience awareness

- describe your own writing process
- record a progress report
- increase sensitivity to language
- write your own textbook

■ Answers to "Practicing What You've Learned" Exercises

Practicing What You've Learned, p. 18

A. 1. This subject is far too broad. It might be narrowed by defining the university's role in a specific field, such as researching solar energy for use in homes.
 2. This subject could be adequately treated in a short essay.
 3. Because of the number of Shakespearean characters, this subject is too large. It might be narrowed to one or two characters of one play.
 4. Obviously, this subject covers too much ground.
 5. A short paper might give a satisfactory overview of this hobby, but for a better essay the student might focus on some specific aspect, such as "how to find rare/older cards," "how to assess the value of a baseball card," or "types of baseball cards."
 6. This subject could be discussed in a short essay, though again the student might profit from focusing on some specific aspect or particular kind of gun control laws—the state/city they govern.
 7. The most serious disadvantages would be covered in a short paper.
 8. The various models and functions of computers are a complex subject, too broad for a brief essay.
 9. This subject could be described adequately.
 10. Once the subject is narrowed to a specific type of bike (e.g., mountain, road, touring), selecting a bicycle would be a good topic for a process paper.

B. You will, of course, receive a variety of suitable answers here. Be sure that the students narrow the subjects sufficiently instead of stopping halfway. For example, a student might be tempted to narrow "music" to "rock music" or "education" to "college," but these subjects are still too broad for a short essay. Better answers will be more specific: "music" to "Melissa Etheridge's latest album," "education" to "required courses," etc. If done properly, this exercise should show students that selecting and narrowing a subject is the first step to discovering the main purpose of their essays. Once this step is mastered, students should find that formulating a thesis is not the difficult problem they might have imagined.

Practicing What You've Learned, p. 22

A. See Chapter 10.
B. Answers will vary.

Discussion of Assignment

The radio audience will want details about the supposed benefits of Breatharianism, even though the students may be skeptical and probably think Brooks is a phony. All the better then to place themselves in the persona of a gullible consumer, but at the same time to keep the assignment realistic by including some references like "Sure, I know you are probably skeptical," which shows an awareness of an audience that is not composed of complete boobs and which makes the ad more believable.

The parade permit application would try to show that these people are not completely crazy and would not pose a threat to public order. Moreover, this might lead to more business for the community as well as a sense that the town was interested in the health and welfare of its citizens and even the environment.

In the report, students can let go with their criticism and finally write for the side they were probably on all along. Details like a nutritional study showing the bad effects this diet would have on health, a record of Brooks's activity in other states and cities, and some personal testimony from other former Breatharians all would strengthen a case that seems sewed up already, so students will need to remember to do more than just say, "He's obviously guilty; let's leave it at that!"

Chapter 2

The Thesis Statement

p. 31

■ Summary

What Is a Thesis? What Does a "Working Thesis" Do?

Can a "Working Thesis" Change?

Guidelines for Writing a Good Thesis

- state the writer's clearly defined opinion on some subject
- assert one main idea
- have something worthwhile to say
- limit thesis to fit the assignment
- state thesis clearly in specific terms
- locate thesis clearly, often in first or second paragraph

Avoiding Common Errors in Thesis Statements

- don't merely announce or describe your intentions; do state an attitude
- don't clutter a thesis with expressions like "In my opinion"; do be forceful, speak directly and with conviction

- don't be unreasonable or insulting; do avoid irresponsible charges, name calling, and profanity
- don't merely state a fact or idea that is self-evident or dead-ended
- don't express a thesis in the form of a question

Practicing What You've Learned, p. 39

Using the Essay Map

Assignment

Practicing What You've Learned, p. 42

Assignment

■ Answers to "Practicing What You've Learned" Exercises

Practicing What You've Learned, p. 39

A. 1. Inadequate. It is unnecessary to say "I think," and "interesting" is too broad to have much meaning. What is it about the movie that is interesting—the subject, the acting, the cinematography? A good thesis is more specific.

  2. Inadequate. First, a thesis should be expressed in a declarative sentence, not in a question. Second, comparing Japanese automobiles to American automobiles is too broad.

  3. Inadequate. This is merely a statement that "some people" have this opinion. The purpose of a paper on this subject, however, is to reveal and support the author's opinion. Moreover "bad" is simply too subjective, not specific; still, it does provide for the heuristic question "In which ways?"

  4. Inadequate. "My essay will tell you" is an announcement.

  5. Adequate. This specific assertion will lead to a discussion of the reasons why final examinations should be given before the winter break.

  6. Inadequate. It is not necessary to mention that the tuition increase will be a "terrible" burden. This thesis also has two parts that need to be separated: what, exactly, the extra burden of a tuition increase is, and what that has to do with the quality of education.

  7. Inadequate. The writer's point is unclear. Does she believe body piercing should be illegal, or is it merely unsightly? It is also unclear whether the writer is unable to look people in the face who are "into body piercing" or if she finds facial piercing particularly offensive.

  8. Inadequate. This statement, while forceful, goes too far. Changing "will" to "could" would allow for a more reasonable tone.

  9. Adequate.

  10. Inadequate. The phrase "very important" is too vague. The thesis should assert a specific idea, such as "Having a close friend you can talk to makes adjusting to dorm living a lot easier."

B. These weak or faulty theses may be rewritten in a variety of ways; the comments below are intended to help you identify the problem with each example.

1. "Negative experience" is too broad; students should substitute specific descriptions.
2. The word "fun" is too subjective—why is it fun? As a counterpoint, "expensive and dangerous" are equally subjective terms. Nevertheless, a longer essay could accommodate definition, comparison, and contrast easily, but the writer would clearly need to set criteria for the subjective terms.
3. This is a "so what?" thesis. Students should either take a stand on the issue or state why it is important for the reader to know the advantages and disadvantages.
4. "One big headache" is too vague.
5. Students should omit the phrase "In this paper I will debate." Also, the writer's position should be clear.
6. Too vague. What is it we need to do about billboard clutter?
7. What is missing from this thesis statement is a purpose. Why do the insurance laws need to be rewritten? Which laws?
8. Too vague. In what ways is it good for the rider?
9. "In my opinion" can be deleted, and "fantastic" is too vague.
10. Too broad. What effects did the Civil Rights movement have? Were they positive or negative? Both?

Practicing What You've Learned, p. 42

A. 1. because of its . . . innovative editing.
2. Such a move . . . highway maintenance.
3. To guarantee . . . personalized design.
4. because it's . . . more luxurious.
5. To qualify . . . and training.
6. Through . . . squads.
7. Because . . . fatty tissue.
8. deductions . . . will be taxed.
9. They're . . . fun to grow.
10. His spirit of protest . . . arrangements.
B. Student responses will vary.

Discussion of Assignments

Answers will vary.

If you have computer facilities available to you, the following practice provides an opportunity for use. Students naturally gravitate to discussion in such analyses, so have them e-mail one another with an example from their own lives for two or three of the quotes. Such an exercise will help reinforce the ideas in Chapter 1 relating to audience while also providing a prewrite for the students' own essays. Such an exercise also foregrounds how to borrow material—both the quotations in question and what others have to reveal in their e-mails. In addition, students may begin to see audiences in ways not previously noted.

Chapter 3

The Body Paragraphs

p. 47

■ Summary

Planning the Body of Your Essay

- informal outlines

Composing the Body Paragraphs

The Topic Sentence

- supports the thesis by clearly stating a main point in the discussion
- announces what the paragraph will be about
- controls the subject matter of the paragraph

Focusing Your Topic Sentence

Placing Your Topic Sentence

Practicing What You've Learned, p. 55

Assignment

Applying What You've Learned to Your Writing

Paragraph Development

- include enough supporting information or evidence to make readers understand the topic sentence
- make the information clear and specific
- avoid vague generalities and repetitious ideas

Paragraph Length

- long enough to accomplish its purpose and short enough to be interesting
- avoid the one- or two-sentence paragraph
- divide longish paragraphs at a logical point; use transitional phrases

Practicing What You've Learned, p. 62

Assignment

Applying What You've Learned to Your Writing

Paragraph Unity

- stick to the subject
- unify sentences around a central or main idea—topic sentence
- unify paragraphs around thesis

Practicing What You've Learned, p. 66

Assignment

Applying What You've Learned to Your Writing

Paragraph Coherence

- use a recognizable order of information
  - order of time
  - order of space
  - deductive order
  - inductive order
- use transitional words and phrases
  - examples
  - comparison/contrast
  - sequence
  - results
- repeat key words
- substitute pronouns for key nouns

- use parallelism
- use a variety of transitional devices
- avoid whiplash—maintain coherence

Practicing What You've Learned, p. 74

Paragraph Sequence

- consider logic, effect

Transitions between Paragraphs

- use to link paragraphs, ideas
- vary the type and placement to avoid sounding mechanical and boring

Applying What You've Learned to Your Writing

■ Answers to "Practicing What You've Learned" Exercises

Practicing What You've Learned, p. 55

A. 1. Denim is one of America's . . .
  2. Adlai Stevenson, American statesman . . .
  3. . . . almost every wedding tradition . . . weddings may vary . . . (concluding sentence)
  4. If any of these sound familiar, . . .
  5. In actuality, the most popular instrument . . .
  6. The wonderful tradition . . .

B. Answers will vary.

C. Your students should add topic sentences that resemble the following:

  1. Many brilliant thinkers were not good students.
  2. Most of the inexpensive trinkets sold when Elvis Presley was a popular rock star have now become much more valuable.
  3. While an author's book or play may be respected by the public, the writer in person often receives little appreciation.
  4. Although we tend to think of "record seasons" in terms of victorious teams, losing seasons are also permanently recorded in the annals of football.

D. Student responses will vary.

Practicing What You've Learned, p. 62

A. 1. The extremely vague adjectives (best, interesting, concerned, great) are the first clue that this paragraph is unfocused. The paragraph might target one of Wilson's strengths, then explain and illustrate it. Also, the reader-oriented purpose of this paragraph is puzzling.

2. Here there are generalized complaints about advice columns that are repetitious and go off in several directions. The solution is to focus on one idea, such as that the advice is out of touch with today's world, and then use examples to support this assertion.

3. This is another general survey of the topic that needs more concrete development to make it more coherent and tie it more closely to the topic sentence.

4. The topic sentence here—"Nursing homes are often sad places"—says it all. The rest of the paragraph is merely a repetition of that fact in different words.

5. While the writer has a clear distinction in mind between acquaintances and friends, trite and overused generalities ("being close to you," "sharing intimate things," "happy about being alive") add no real development to the paragraph. Also, using "you" in the hypothetical examples is ineffective; detailed, real, personal, or observed examples would be much more compelling.

B. Answers will vary.

Practicing What You've Learned, p. 66

Delete the following sentences from the sample paragraphs:

1. During this period, songwriters . . .
2. Another well-known incident of cannibalism in the West occurred . . .
3. To publicize his new product . . . (Some readers might also consider the last sentence a break, though it might be seen as additional information to conclude the paragraph.)
4. U.S. Representative from Colorado . . . (to end of paragraph)
5. This example illustrates a drift from the original topic (dorm living providing a good way to meet people) into a new, slightly different topic (new friends teach students to get along with people from foreign countries). The writer might use the friend from Peru as an example of her original position, but overall she needs to rewrite the last half of her paragraph to bring it in line with her topic sentence.

Practicing What You've Learned, p. 74

A. The first paragraph, on the apartment, is ordered by space, with the point of view moving from the left of the front door to the back of the room to the right of the door.

The second paragraph, on acts of greeting, is ordered chronologically, with details selected from the seventeenth-century tip through today.

The third paragraph, on exams, is ordered by parallelism, with sentences structured in the repeated pattern of "synonym for students + verb."

B. The transitional devices in each paragraph are underlined:

1. Each year I follow a system when preparing firewood to use in my stove. First, I hike about a mile from my house with my bow saw in hand. I then select three good size oak trees and mark them with orange ties. Next, I saw through the base of each tree about two feet from the ground. After I fell the trees, not only do I trim away the branches, but I also sort the scrap from the usable limbs. I find cutting the trees into manageable length logs is too much for one day; however, I roll them off the ground so they will not begin to rot. The next day I cut the trees into eight-foot lengths, which allows me to

handle <u>them</u> more easily. <u>Once they</u> are cut, I roll <u>them</u> along the fire lane to the edge of the road where I stack them neatly but not too high. <u>The next day</u> I borrow my uncle's van, drive to the <u>pile of logs</u>, and load as many <u>logs</u> as I can, thus reducing the number of trips. When I finally have all the logs in my backyard, I begin sawing <u>them</u> into eighteen-inch lengths. I create large piles that <u>consequently</u> have to be split and <u>finally</u> stacked. The <u>logs</u> will age and dry until <u>winter</u> when I will make daily trips to the woodpile.

2. Fans of professional baseball and football argue continually over which is America's favorite spectator sport. Though the figures on attendance for <u>each</u> vary with every new season, certain arguments remain the same, spelling out both the enduring appeals of each game and something about the people who love to watch. <u>Football, for instance</u>, is a quicker, more physical <u>sport</u>, and football fans enjoy the emotional involvement <u>they</u> feel while watching. <u>Baseball, on the other hand</u>, seems more mental, like chess, and attracts those <u>fans</u> who prefer a quieter, more complicated <u>game. In addition</u>, professional football teams usually play no more than fourteen <u>games</u> a year, providing fans with a whole week between games to work themselves up to a pitch of excitement and expectation. Baseball teams, <u>however</u>, play almost every day for six months, so that the typical baseball fan is not so crushed by missing a <u>game</u>, knowing there will be many other chances to attend. <u>Finally</u> football fans seem to love the half-time pageantry, the marching bands, and the pretty cheerleaders, <u>whereas</u> baseball <u>fans</u> are more content to concentrate on the <u>game's</u> finer details and spend the breaks between innings filling out their own private scorecards.

C. The choice of transition words may vary slightly from student to student, but here is a typical response to the dinosaur paragraph:

dinosaurs, then, Because, reptiles, however, although, dinosaurs, they, as well as, Another, dinosaurs, In addition, dinosaurs, also, dinosaurs, therefore, monsters, other, scientists, dinosaurs, or.

D. The sentences in paragraph 1 should be grouped in this order: G, H, B, F, D, A, C, E.
The sentences in paragraph 2 should be grouped in this order: F, C, G, I, H, D, B, A, E.

Chapter 4

Beginnings and Endings
p. 79

■ **Summary**

How to Write a Good Lead-in

- a paradoxical or intriguing statement
- an arresting statistic or shocking statement
- a question
- a quotation or literary allusion
- a relevant story, joke, or anecdote
- a description, often used for emotional appeal
- a factual statement or summary who-what-where-when-why lead-in
- an analogy or comparison
- a contrast
- a personal experience
- a catalog of relevant examples
- a statement of a problem or a popular misconception
- a brief dialogue to introduce the topic
- a proverb, maxim, or motto
- a recognition, revelation, or insight

Avoiding Errors in Lead-ins

- make sure your lead-in introduces your thesis
- keep lead-in brief
- don't begin with an apology or complaint
- don't assume your audience already knows your subject matter
- stay clear of overused lead-ins

Practicing What You've Learned, p. 83

Assignment

How to Write a Good Concluding Paragraph

- a restatement of both the thesis and the essay's major points
- an evaluation of the importance of the essay's subject
- a statement of the essay's broader implications
- a call to action
- a prophecy or warning based on the essay's thesis
- a witticism that emphasizes or sums up the point of the essay
- a quotation that emphasizes or sums up the point of the essay
- an image or description that lends finality to the essay
- a rhetorical question that makes the reader think about the essay's main point
- a forecast based on the essay's thesis
- a return to a technique used in your lead-in

Avoiding Errors in Conclusions

- avoid a mechanical ending
- don't introduce new points
- don't tack on a conclusion
- don't change your stance
- avoid trite expressions
- don't insult or anger your reader

Practicing What You've Learned, p. 88

Assignment

How to Write a Good Title

- attracts readers' interest
- announces the tone of the essay
- suggests content
- is not underlined or put in quotation marks
- is capitalized according to MLA guidelines
- clarifies scope and/or tone of essay

Practicing What You've Learned, p. 89

Assignment

Applying What You've Learned to Your Writing

■ Answers to "Practicing What You've Learned" Exercises

Practicing What You've Learned, p. 83

Student responses will vary, but it should be noted that each example uses more than one type of lead-in: 1) uses a quote and an anecdote; 2) uses a question and a factual statement; 3) uses a factual statement, an arresting statistic, and a contrast; 4) uses a story, an analogy, and a personal experience; and 5) uses a factual summary of an event and an intriguing statement.

Practicing What You've Learned, p. 88

Again, student responses will vary. Here, however, example number one is too mechanical, even though it reiterates the thesis and main points. Number two introduces new points/topics and number three is just plain insulting.

Practicing What You've Learned, p. 89

Responses will vary.

Chapter 5

Drafting and Revising: Creative Thinking, Critical Thinking

p. 91

■ Summary

What Is Revision?

- revision is a thinking process

When Does Revision Occur?

- revision occurs throughout the writing process

Myths about Revision

- revision is not autopsy
- revision is not limited to editing or proofreading
- revision is not punishment or busywork

Can I Learn to Improve My Revision Skills?

Preparing to Draft: Some Time-Saving Hints

- if handwriting drafts, use only one side of the paper
- leave big margins on both sides of each page for additional information
- devise a system of symbols to remind you of changes you want to make later
- leave blank spots to note areas needing further development
- use a line or x for corrections or potential deletions; don't scratch out original material completely
- try to work from a typed copy
- always try to keep notes, outlines, drafts, and an extra copy of your final paper

Additional Suggestions for Writers with Word Processors

- save your work regularly and print a copy of every draft
- learn to use the editing tools of your software, but don't rely on spell-checkers
- use the search command to sweep for commonly made errors
- read printed versions of your text to see what your readers will see

Writing Centers, Computer Labs, and Computer Classrooms

A Revision Process for Your Drafts

I. Revising for Purpose, Thesis, and Audience

- fulfill assignment objectives
- follow directions carefully
- understand the purpose of your essay
- comprehend your audience—put a face to it
- select appropriate strategies for your goal

II. Revising for Ideas and Evidence

- relate major points to thesis
- focus a position
- use effective and relevant points
- state and locate points clearly

What Is Critical Thinking?

- the ability to analyze and evaluate your own ideas and those of others

Thinking Critically as a Writer

- learn to distinguish fact from opinion

- support your own opinions with evidence
- evaluate the strength of your evidence
- use enough specific supporting evidence
- watch for biases and strong emotions that may undermine evidence
- check evidence for logical fallacies

III. Revising for Organization

- use an appropriate strategy for your purpose
- order points logically
- use clear topic sentences
- use transitions between paragraphs
- proportion ideas for effectiveness
- use an effective title and lead-in
- conclude thoughtfully, emphatically, or memorably
- don't be hesitant to restructure drafts

IV. Revising for Clarity and Style

- check for clear, precise sentences
- avoid wordiness
- provide a variety of sentence lengths
- check for appropriate word choices
- use active verbs and lively language
- eliminate jargon, clichés, and pretentious language
- use an authentic voice

V. Editing for Errors

- read aloud
- know your enemies/your own weaknesses in punctuation/grammar
- read backwards
- learn some "tricks" for punctuation/grammar problems
- eliminate diction and mechanical errors readers find annoying
- use your tools (reference texts such as dictionary, thesaurus, handbook)

VI. Proofreading

- set work aside for a time; review with "fresh eyes"
- freshen pages for a "professional look"

A Final Checklist for Your Essay

Practicing What You've Learned, p. 106

Benefiting from Revision Workshops

As writer:

- develop a constructive attitude
- come prepared
- evaluate suggestions carefully
- find the good in bad advice

As reader:

- develop a constructive attitude
- be clear and specific
- address important issues
- encourage the writer
- understand your role as a critical reader

Practicing What You've Learned, p. 111

Assignment

Some Last Advice: How to Play with Your Mental Blocks

- give yourself as much time as possible to write your essay
- verbalize ideas
- break paper into manageable bits
- get the juices flowing and the pen moving
- set reasonable limits of time for writing to prevent anxiety
- give yourself permission to write garbage
- warm up by writing something easier
- imagine writing to a friend
- remember that writer's block is temporary
- if you have a bright idea for one section, move to it or jot it down
- reconnect with your subject matter
- do something else for a while
- relax, and remember that no one writes perfectly every time

■ Answers to "Practicing What You've Learned" Exercises

Practicing What You've Learned, p. 106

Answers will vary.

Practicing What You've Learned, p. 111

These two essays lend themselves to a variety of assignments. The students might mark them at home and then discuss them in class, rewrite them on the board or in groups, or rewrite them individually at home. The comments below are intended for use as guidelines, not as a complete set of corrections.

A. "Maybe You Shouldn't Go Away to College"

This student needs help with organization, paragraph development and unity, and sentence construction. The comparison of the local school to the out-of-town school should be made much clearer in each body paragraph through the addition of specific examples.

Paragraph 1: The thesis is clear but the essay map is expressed awkwardly.

Paragraph 2: The contrast between the cost of attending an out-of-town college and living at home needs a clearer statement in the topic sentence. How can the writer know that out-of-town colleges always have higher tuition? Perhaps it would be more effective to discuss the expense of transportation rather than tuition, which varies from school to school regardless of location. The example of room and board should be developed further.

Paragraph 3: This sentence seems off the subject; omit the paragraph.

Paragraph 4: This paragraph does have a point, but the writer needs to focus and clarify what kinds of "changes" she means. Development of the paragraph should be improved by adding some specific examples of the pressures and changes involved in going away to college; the writer could then show how the security of home could make such changes easier.

Paragraphs 5 and 6: These two paragraphs discuss the same point and therefore need to be combined. However, instead of merely asking whether students should be forced to break away at this time, the writer should persuasively argue her own position, perhaps by explaining some of the responsibilities of going away to college. (She also needs to make sure that her discussion of "responsibilities" does not merely repeat the discussion of "pressures" in paragraph 4. Are these two points really different? If they aren't, her essay map also needs rethinking.)

Paragraph 7: The conclusion is unnecessarily brief, although the writer does try to end with a play on words ("right road" and "just around the corner").

B. Letter to Mom and Dad

The writer's basic concept of audience is flawed even though the audience is well known. The content suggests a number of difficulties for which the writer will need cash, but does not promise context for any of those difficulties. The writer needs to fill in details, explain circumstances, appeal to his parents' reason and emotion, and provide them with a clear reason or several reasons why they should continue to support him and/or not yank him out of school.

Before these concerns are handled, however, the writer should begin by prioritizing needs. What does the writer most need and why—legal assistance or cash? The writer should consider eliminating any details not related to reasons for his request, such as the "rash" and the girlfriend's tattoos and body piercings.

This writer may need help developing ideas through successive drafts, but once the material is revised, he should then proofread for spelling errors and fragments.

Chapter 6

Effective Sentences

p. 117

■ Summary

Developing a Clear Style

- give your sentences content
- make your sentences specific
- avoid overpacking your sentences
- fix fragments
- pay attention to word order
- avoid mixed constructions and faulty predication

Practicing What You've Learned, p. 125

Developing a Concise Style

- avoid deadwood constructions
- avoid redundancy
- carefully consider your passive verbs
- avoid pretentiousness

Practicing What You've Learned, p. 131

Assignment

Developing a Lively Style

- use specific, descriptive verbs
- use specific, precise modifiers that help the reader see, hear, or feel what you are describing
- emphasize people when possible
- vary your sentence style
- avoid overuse of any one kind of construction in the same sentence
- don't change your point of view between or within sentences

Practicing What You've Learned, p. 136

Developing an Emphatic Style

- word order
- coordination
- subordination

Practicing What You've Learned, p. 140

Assignment

Applying What You've Learned to Your Writing

■ Answers to "Practicing What You've Learned" Exercises

Practicing What You've Learned, p. 125
Some suggestions follow:

A. 1. Roger's marketing skills made him important to his company's sales department.
   2. The new detective show on TV stars Phil Noir and is set in the 1940s.
   3. I can't help but wonder if he is welcome.
   4. *Biofeedback: How to Stop It* has so many funny and sarcastic comments about California self-help fads, I couldn't put it down.
   5. The floor of Sarah's room was always cluttered with dolls, clothes, game pieces, books, and old candy wrappers.
   6. Are you afraid poor auto repair service will ruin your next road trip? Come to the Fix-It Shop for expert care; we'll replace worn parts on your car for your peace of mind.
   7. At my local college, I've signed up for a class in "Cultivating Mold in Your Refrigerator for Fun and Profit."
   8. Your horoscope may not be accurate, but reading it can be entertaining.
   9. Lois Mueller, the author of *The Underachiever's Guide to Very Small Business Opportunities* and *Whine Your Way to Success,* is having an autograph party at the campus bookstore today at noon.

10. Upon being asked if she would like to live forever, one contestant in the 1994 Miss USA contest replied that she would if she could, but she can't.

B. 1. Go to the police to learn ways to avoid being accosted in the subway.
2. Escorted down the aisle by her father, the bride wore an antique wedding gown—a family heirloom.
3. I miss my dog even though it has been dead almost five years now.
4. For sale: Unique handmade gifts for that special person in your life.
5. After putting off surgery for years, I finally had my leg operated on.
6. We need to hire two nonsmoking teachers for the preschool kids.
7. The story of Rip Van Winkle illustrates the dangers of oversleeping.
8. We gave our waterbed to our friends.
9. Neither people who are allergic to chocolate nor children under six should be given the new vaccine.
10. At 7 a.m., Kate starts preparing for another busy day as an executive.

Practicing What You've Learned, p. 131

1. He lost the editing job because of his careless and sloppy proofreading.
2. Staff members noted that many at the company picnic threw their trash on the ground.
3. My older brother can't drive to work this week because he wrecked his car early Saturday morning.
4. Today, we often criticize advertising that demeans women or represents them unfairly.
5. The defense attorney objected to the prosecutor's attempt to introduce the antique gun.
6. In "Now Is the Winter of Our Discount Tent," the poet expresses her disgust with camping.
7. Although the boss appeared to be listening, we didn't think she took our concerns seriously.
8. Learning word processing makes you more efficient.
9. Some people assert their superiority by being rude.
10. To improve my chances for promotion, I wooed the boss's daughter.

Practicing What You've Learned, p. 136

A. 1. After listening to the whining moan of the reactor, I'm not sure that nuclear power has a future.
2. The City Council members were embarrassed because the application forms for grants were mailed without stamps.
3. Watching Jim Bob eat pork chops was nauseating.
4. For sale: elegant antique bureau.
5. Let's all enjoy ourselves!
6. My roommate may be eccentric but he's loyal to his friends.
7. After reading "The Looter's Guide to Riot-Prone Cities," Eddie requested an immediate transfer.
8. The wild oats soup was so delicious we slurped it all down in five minutes.

9. Warren Peace threw his new cat, Chairman Meow, in the air when it won 1st place in the pet show.
10. The new diet gave me headaches and leg cramps.

Practicing What You've Learned, p. 140

A. 1. Joe Louis, one-time heavyweight boxing champion, once said, "I don't really like money but it quiets my nerves."
   2. Recent polls suggest that most Americans get their news from television.
   3. Of all the world's problems, the most urgent is hunger.
   4. Of all the foreign countries I visited last year, my favorite was Greece.
   5. One habit I will not tolerate is knuckle-cracking.

B. 1. The guru rejected his dentist's offer of novocaine because he could transcend dental medication.
   2. Because John incorrectly identified Harper Lee as the author of the south-of-the-border classic *Tequila Mockingbird,* he failed his literature test.
   3. She pressed "9" but when she couldn't find an "11" on the dial, Peggy Sue's house burned.
   4. Although the police had only a few clues, they suspected that Jean and David had strangled each other in a desperate struggle over control of the thermostat.
   5. Described by one critic as a "pinhead chiller," *Sorority Babes in the Slimeball Bowl-o-rama* (1988) is Bubba's favorite movie.
   6. Because their menu includes banana split personality, repressed duck, shrimp basket case, and self-expresso, we're going to the Psychoanalysis Restaurant.
   7. Kato lost the junior high spelling bee when he couldn't spell *DNA.*
   8. Colorado hosts an annual BobFest to honor all persons named Bob, and events include playing softbob, bobbing for apples, listening to bob-pipes, and eating bob-e-que.
   9. When the earthquake shook the city, Louise was performing primal-scream therapy. (Or: Because Louise was performing primal-scream therapy, an earthquake shook the city!)
   10. In 1789 many Parisians bought a new perfume called "Guillotine" because they wanted to be on the cutting edge of fashion.

C. Obviously, the sentences may be combined in many ways. Here are some examples.
   1. While living on a raft on the Mississippi River, a runaway boy, accompanied by an escaped slave, has many adventures and learns valuable lessons about friendship and human kindness.
   2. A young man returning from prison joins his family in their move from the Dust Bowl to California, where they find intolerance and dishonest employers instead of jobs.
   3. A mad scientist who wants to re-create life makes a gruesome monster in his laboratory but is killed by his rebellious creature as the villagers, in revolt, storm the castle.

Chapter 7

Word Logic
p. 145

■ Summary

Selecting the Correct Words

Accuracy

- confused words
- idiomatic phrases

Levels of Language

- colloquial
- informal
- formal

Tone

- invective
- sarcasm
- irony
- flippancy or cuteness

- sentimentality
- preachiness
- pomposity

Connotation and Denotation

- emotional association versus literal meaning

Practicing What You've Learned, p. 151

Selecting the Best Words

- make them as precise as possible
- make them as fresh and original as possible
- don't use trendy expressions or slang
- select simple, direct words your readers can easily understand
- call things by their proper names
- avoid sexist language
- enliven your writing with figurative language when appropriate
- vary your word choice so that your prose does not sound wordy, repetitious, or monotonous
- remember that wordiness is a major problem for all writers, even professionals

Practicing What You've Learned, p. 163

Assignment

Applying What You've Learned to Your Writing

■ Answers to "Practicing What You've Learned" Exercises

Practicing What You've Learned, p. 151

A. 1. two weeks, two friends, too short, too tired, you're, too broke
2. who's, photographic, accepted, number, compliments
3. It's, too, their, generic, they're, rolls, your
4. foul
5. regardless, course, vain
6. Ants
7. lose, your, metal, its
8. council, affect

B. 1. The sunset signaled the cat to come out for its nightly prowl.
2. "You're fired" may tempt students, but it, too, seems unreasonable. Ask them to consider other options such as, "We no longer require your services, thank you."

3. I wanted information about the poor.
4. If the bill to legalize marijuana is passed, we think most Americans will soon be smoking it.
5. I enjoy watching white mice.

C. The word with the most pleasing connotation is on the left, the least pleasing on the right. Opinions may vary.

1. serene/boring
2. slender/anorexic
3. famous/notorious
4. affluent/privileged
5. educator/lecturer

D. 1. aroma
2. voluptuous single woman, bargains
3. strict
4. concern
5. expert, presentation, older gentleman
6. unusual
7. competent
8. distinctive, unemployed
9. religious beliefs
10. led

Practicing What You've Learned, p. 163

A. Everyone, of course, will have different responses, but here are some suggestions:

1. The chemical experiment killed all the fish in the river.
2. The guest speaker's references to religious cults were inappropriate for a prom banquet.
3. The 50-room mausoleum was rotting away and covered with tacky trim and ornaments.
4. Our father likes to spend time helping us and entertaining us with stories from his childhood.
5. Sandbagging our riverfront property was exhausting, but it brought the neighbors closer together.
6. My new lawnmower came without a handle and wheels.
7. Mother Teresa was more dedicated than most of us to helping the poor.
8. The biology textbook lacked a lively voice.
9. I could hear the baby screaming a block away.
10. For only three dollars we got eighteen appetizers, five main courses, and fifteen desserts at the Yugoslavian restaurant.

B. 1. When the flight attendant didn't return from the bathroom, we were worried.
2. Any new congressional member for our state must comprehend the financial potential of tourism.
3. All eligible voters should vote during every election.
4. I thought the $250 rebate on a new set of tires was worth the purchase of a certain brand, but my sister wasn't convinced.
5. Farmers may be forced to sell their farms, move to town, and go on welfare.

6. Both Ron Howard and Shirley Temple were successful child actors. As adults they continued their success in different ways: Howard began directing movies and Temple served as a U.S. ambassador to Ghana and Czechoslovakia.
7. Each president realizes that war means killing people.
8. Although Jack once thought Jill was sincere, he soon realized she was not.
9. The City Councilman was furious to learn that his son had been arrested for embezzling funds from the low-income housing project.
10. The automobile company sent a letter to all Gator X42 owners praising the car's vinyl interior, but warning that the X42 had been recalled because its defective steering system could cause the driver to lose control of the vehicle.

C. 1. For good health, use a toothpick daily and avoid tanning salons.
2. According to the military, you should not attempt a predawn jump without a parachute from an airplane because you would crash into the ground. (This is only a best guess; some jargon is so convoluted that any number of interpretations is possible.)
3. American Airlines passengers can now take a shuttle to and from their flights.
4. If you are in the military, you should avoid being shot and killed.
5. The U.S. Embassy in Budapest warned its employees that friendly local women might actually be Hungarian agents.
6. At a 2003 press conference on the war in Iraq, Defense Secretary Donald Rumsfeld evaded questions, somewhat unsuccessfully.
7. The employee was fired because she was rude and lazy.
8. In 2005, President George W. Bush called for accountability in public schools nationwide.
9. All of us could understand Mabel's essay on the effect of the decreased tax base on funding for education.
10. According to Admiral Wesley L. MacDonald, U.S. intelligence was not monitoring action in Grenada until just prior to the United States' 1983 invasion.

Discussion of Assignment

The exercises in this chapter provide an opportunity to begin blending rhetorical goals with stylistic ones. One option is to have students type up alternate versions of individual paragraphs and share them with others in their group. Give them time to discuss each other's changes and then combine paragraphs in a unified whole. This assignment could be done on e-mail or through HyperNews or any share-type software as either an in-class or homework assignment. This option will require students to consider the linguistic features they alter while collaborating to produce a written product, rather than merely generating ideas or making stylistic changes in the abstract.

A. Responses will necessarily vary, but the essential shifts are suggested below.

Total preparation time: 35 minutes

Ingredients:

(list is fine)

Directions:

Preheat oven to 375 degrees.

In a large bowl, measure and mix together first six ingredients. In a separate bowl, sift together flour, baking soda, and salt; then fully blend with the wet ingredients. Fold in chocolate pieces and nuts.

Drop mixture by teaspoonfuls onto ungreased baking sheet about 2 inches apart. Bake 8–10 minutes. Remove and cool.

B. Again, answers will vary. Some students will provide silly or nonsense responses on purpose. The idea here is not so much to be logical, but to discover the intertwining of syntax and meaning. Some traditional responses might be as follows:

> crept, dark, impending, sports, been abandoned, moonlit, jumped, fear, shrieks, climbed, broken, front, freezing, leaves, scary, knocked, aged, mask, stared, laughed.

C. Responses will vary.

Chapter 8

The Reading-Writing Connection

p. 169

▪ Summary

How Can Reading Well Help Me Become a Better Writer?

How Can I Become an Analytical Reader?

Steps to Reading Well

- before reading the essay, note publication information and biographical data on the author
- note the title of the essay
- read the essay—noting any key ideas and referring to the dictionary as desired—then briefly summarize your impression of the essay
- review the title and introductory paragraphs again
- locate and mark the thesis
- locate and mark supporting points or ideas
- note how the writer develops, explains, or argues each supporting point
- practice using marginal symbols to mark points of interest

- review the essay's organization
- review the unity and coherence of the essay, noting transitions
- consider the writer's style and the essay's tone

Sample Annotated Essay: "Our Youth Should Serve"—Steven Muller

Practicing What You've Learned, p. 175

Assignment

Writing a Summary

- read selection carefully and annotate
- when drafting, include the title and author's name in first sentence
- use your own words
- omit references to examples, strategies, and supporting details
- use quotation marks for text that you must borrow
- do not give your own opinion; be objective, accurate, and concise

Practicing What You've Learned, p. 177

Benefiting from Class Discussions

- try to arrive a few minutes early and review your reading and notes
- remind yourself to become an "active listener"
- turn off pagers, cell phones, and other electronic devices
- listen carefully to your classmates' opinions, offer your own insights, and be willing to voice agreement or polite disagreement
- ask questions or request additional information when necessary for your understanding
- practice thinking critically on two levels: of the essay under review as a draft in which the writer made choices and as an example for ways or reasons to revise your own writing
- take notes and listen for verbal cues to essential material
- develop or borrow a shorthand method for note-taking
- attend every class session and participate actively

■ Answers to "Practicing What You've Learned" Exercises

Practicing What You've Learned, p. 175
Student responses will vary.

Practicing What You've Learned, p. 177
Student responses will vary.

Discussion

Have students share summaries online to see who can write the most concise version of the summaries assigned as practice on page 177. Let them borrow/steal from each other but follow the rules for summary in relation to published material. They will see how much they steal and they will be able to make better judgments about how to incorporate material without "cheating." They should also be alerted to the fact that plagiarism is theft and that even though you gave them permission to steal from each other for the sake of learning from the assignment, such an act committed without permission from the author, classmate or not, would always otherwise be considered an act of plagiarism. Don't be surprised if students anticipate this idea when you tell them they can steal from each other for this assignment and consider it unfair. A variation here may be to see who can write the most concise version without stealing from his or her neighbor!

Part 2

Purposes, Modes, and Strategies

■ **Part Two Summary p. 181**

Exposition by Example, Process Analysis, Comparison/ Contrast, Definition, Division/Classification, and Causal Analysis

   ▪ intends to explain or inform

Argumentation

   ▪ intends to convince or persuade

Description

   ▪ intends to create a word picture of a person, place, object, or feeling

Narration

   ▪ intends to tell a story or recount an event

Writing Essays Using Multiple Strategies

C h a p t e r 9

Exposition
p. 183

■ Summary

The Strategies of Exposition

Strategy One: Development by Example

- examples support, clarify, interest, and persuade
- examples can be brief
- examples can be extended
- examples can explain and clarify
- examples can be used in all types of writing

Developing Your Essay

- select relevant examples
- select strong and convincing examples
- select enough to make each point clear and persuasive

Problems to Avoid

- a lack of specific detail
- a lack of coherence

Essay Topics

A Topic Proposal for Your Essay

- identify subject of your essay and your attitude toward it
- state a reason for your topic choice
- identify your audience(s)
- state your purpose for writing
- list some examples to use for development
- identify potential problems; narrow and refine your focus

Sample Student Essay

Professional Essay

Questions on Content, Structure, and Style, p. 195

Suggestions for Writing

Vocabulary

Reviewing Your Progress

Strategy Two: Development by Process Analysis

Directional versus Informative

Developing Your Essay

- select an appropriate subject
- describe any necessary equipment
- define special terms
- state steps in a logical, chronological order
- explain each step clearly, sufficiently, accurately
- organize steps effectively

Problems to Avoid

- don't forget to include a thesis
- pay special attention to the conclusion

Essay Topics

A Topic Proposal for Your Essay

- identify your subject as either directional or informative

- determine your subject's complexity
- state a reason for your topic choice
- identify your audience(s)
- identify your purpose
- list at least three steps or stages in the process
- identify potential problems

Sample Student Essay

Professional Essays

- I. The Informative Process Essay

Questions on Content, Structure, and Style, p. 210

Suggestions for Writing

Vocabulary

- II. The Directional Process Essay

Questions on Content, Structure, and Style, p. 213

Suggestions for Writing

Vocabulary

Reviewing Your Progress

Strategy Three: Development by Comparison and Contrast

Developing Your Essay

- point-by-point pattern
- block pattern

Which Pattern Should You Use?

- audition both patterns in the prewriting stage

Problems to Avoid

- the "so what?" thesis is the most serious error
- describe your subjects clearly and distinctly
- avoid a choppy essay

Essay Topics

A Topic Proposal for Your Essay

- identify the two subjects and some ways in which they are similar/different
- determine whether to compare or contrast
- determine your purpose
- identify your audience(s)
- list three or four points of comparison or contrast
- identify potential problems, including the "so what?" factor

Sample Student Essays

- I. The Point-by-Point Pattern
- II. The Block Pattern

Professional Essays

- I. The Point-by-Point Pattern

Questions on Content, Structure, and Style, p. 230

Suggestions for Writing

Vocabulary

- II. The Block Pattern

Questions on Content, Structure, and Style, p. 232

Suggestions for Writing

Vocabulary

A Revision Worksheet

A Special Kind of Comparison: The Analogy

A comparison that uses one thing to clarify or argue a second thing

- use to clarify and explain
- use to argue and persuade or to help support an idea
- use to dramatize or capture an image

Problems to Avoid

- don't use trite, unclear, or illogical analogies
- don't substitute an analogy for other kinds of evidence to support points of an argument
- don't use analogies as "scare tactics"

Reviewing Your Progress

Strategy Four: Development by Definition

Dictionary versus Humorous versus Extended

Why Do We Define?

We define

- to clarify the abstract
- to provide personal interpretation of the vague, controversial, or misunderstood
- to explain the new or unusual (slang, dialect, or jargon)
- to make understandable the unfamiliar
- to offer information to a particular audience
- to inform or entertain by presenting a word's interesting history, uses, or effects

Developing Your Essay

- know your purpose
- give your readers a reason to read
- keep your audience in mind to anticipate and avoid problems of clarity
- use as many strategies as necessary to clarify your definition

    1. describe parts or categories
    2. state examples
    3. compare/contrast similarities
    4. explain a process
    5. provide familiar synonyms
    6. define by negation
    7. trace history/development or changes from original linguistic meaning
    8. discuss causes or effects
    9. identify times/places of use
    10. associate with recognizable people, places, or ideas

Problems to Avoid

Don't:

- present an incomplete definition
- introduce your essay with a quotation from *Webster's*
- define vaguely or by using generalities
- offer circular definitions

Essay Topics

A Topic Proposal for Your Essay

- identify your subject and determine whether to define it subjectively or objectively
- state a reason for your topic choice
- identify your audience(s)

- determine your purpose
- list at least two techniques to help you define terms
- identify potential problems

Sample Student Essay

Professional Essay

Questions on Content, Structure, and Style, p. 247

Suggestions for Writing

Vocabulary

A Revision Worksheet

Reviewing Your Progress

Strategy Five: Development by Division and Classification

- Division is the act of separating something into its component parts
- Classification is the systematic grouping of a number of things into categories

Developing Your Essay

- select one principle of classification or division and stick to it
- state the purpose of your division or classification
- account for all the parts in your division or classification

Problems to Avoid

- underdeveloped categories
- indistinct categories
- too few or too many categories

Essay Topics

A Topic Proposal for Your Essay

- identify your subject and determine whether to classify or divide
- determine which principle of classification or division to use
- state a reason for your topic choice
- identify your audience(s)
- list at least three categories for development
- identify potential problems

Strategy Six: Development by Causal Analysis

Cause is the condition that produces something; it asks, "Why does/did/will X happen?"
Effect is the result produced by something; it asks, "What does/did/will Y produce?"

Developing Your Essay

- present a reasonable thesis statement
- limit your essay to a discussion of recent, major causes or effects
- organize your essay clearly
- convince your reader that a causal relationship exists by showing how the relationship works

Problems to Avoid

- don't oversimplify
- avoid the *post hoc* fallacy
- avoid circular logic

Essay Topics

A Topic Proposal for Your Essay

- identify your subject and purpose; narrow subject and focus
- determine your method of development

- state a reason for your topic choice
- identify your audience(s)
- list at least two major causes or effects
- identify potential problems

Sample Student Essay

Professional Essay

Questions on Content, Structure, and Style, p. 273

Suggestions for Writing

Vocabulary

A Revision Worksheet

Reviewing Your Progress

■ Discussion, Answers to Questions, Vocabulary

1. Example

"So What's So Bad About Being So-So?" by Lisa Wilson Strick—p. 193

Discussion

Strick's essay, originally published in 1984, appeared at a time of heightened awareness of the competitiveness of American society. Do college students today still perceive overzealous competition as a problem in the United States? A lively discussion could result by asking students to agree or disagree with Strick's contention that "in today's competitive world we have to be 'experts.'" Ask them to support their views with specific examples in the same manner that Strick supports her thesis. Consider having students compare this essay to Zinsser's "College Pressures." How do the essays complement each other? Do students agree with the combined views of these writers?

Answers to Questions, p. 195

1. It is an example that introduces the thesis.
2. The thesis is implied throughout the essay, but is stated clearly and without equivocation in the next-to-last paragraph: "I think it's time we put a stop to all this . . . and . . . enjoy being a beginner again." Our many leisure-time activities were meant to be enjoyed, not necessarily mastered.
3. The major examples are from sports; perhaps more could have been offered from school. The first, running, refers to the pervasive concern for and availability of equipment. In this case, it is the right shoes, another area of specialization that wasn't a concern in the old days when anything to protect your feet would do. The dancing example continues

the emphasis on the proper costume, the correct look, for specialized activities. The next three, knitting, soccer, and lessons, illustrate the effect of competition on attitudes rather than externals.

4. Too much competition drains the fun out of an experience. Her piano playing irritates her son, running without the proper equipment is an embarrassment to serious athletes, "real" dancers don't just mess around with a few steps, and "if children can't attain a high level of expertise in soccer, gymnastics, and foreign languages, it is as if their time and effort were wasted. Children don't seem to be able to have fun anymore, as reflected by the daughter in paragraph 8 who muses, "Well, I don't actually have a lot of free time."

5. In paragraph 4, informal verbs like "pulling on" your sneakers and "slogging" are in contrast to formal ones like "plan" and "log." In addition, the mention of "leather or canvas," the type of sole, and the brand of shoe are nice contrasts to her image of an earlier time when a concern for such fine points was unnecessary. Paragraph 6 has a long sentence full of details about the reindeer sweater. The form of the sentence reinforces the point Strick is making about how general knowledge is not sufficient; these days you have to add all sorts of little touches that demonstrate your great skill. A sentence in paragraph 8 is similar, only this time the subject is early childhood education; in addition to soccer lessons at age three, Strick throws in parenthetical references to preschool diving, creative writing, and Suzuki clarinet. All three refer to early education, but the examples Strick chooses seem frivolous or unnecessary and reinforce the sarcastic tone of her essay. Most of the other paragraphs have a similar depth and breadth of detail.

6. Dialogue makes the points of the essay more real and personal. It's fine to criticize a lifestyle, but maybe the author is overly picky or is isolated from mainstream, middle-of-the road culture. Quotations from real people tend to soften this impression and give the essay the feel of a documentary.

7. The solution is to take up an activity without ever intending to become good at it. This change in attitude seems naive and yet at the same time a relief from the competitive atmosphere Strick has described. Strick uses the example of two-year-olds to give adults an idea of how to change their attitude and get on the road to a so-so lifestyle. Presumably, two-year-olds have not yet been infected with that competitive spirit.

8. Although there are many occasions when Strick is humorous, overall the tone of the essay is that of a person who is genuinely concerned about the way we live our lives and wants us to change our habits. She uses phrases like "Have you noticed?" or "We used to do these things for fun," and she even acknowledges that what she is criticizing has some merit ("Ambition, drive and the desire to excel are all admirable within limits"), all of which gives her suggestions and point of view credibility. Since this is not a scholarly treatise intended for presentation at a conference of sociology professors, the breezy informality of the piece will be more interesting to a general reader. Also, since many of these readers are deeply affected by the lifestyle Strick describes, her gently humorous but pointed comments are more likely to be taken seriously; Strick seems to be the neighbor we all have or are, and we share her concerns as well as her frustration.

9. The conclusion wraps up the essay by putting into practice (not too much, of course!) the process Strick has just suggested: take up an activity with no intention of becoming good at it.

10. Student agreement/disagreement should be well supported with specific textual examples.

Vocabulary

1. errant (2)—roving, straying, wandering
2. incompetence (3)—lack of necessary ability
3. aficionados (4)—enthusiastic admirers or followers
4. mediocrity (4)—average to below-average ability
5. excel (9)—to surpass or do better than others
6. fluent (9)—flowing smoothly or gracefully; most often used to describe those who speak and write foreign languages well
7. zest (11)—spirited enjoyment; gusto

2. Process Analysis: Informative

"To Bid the World Farewell" by Jessica Mitford—p. 207

Discussion

Mitford's essay shows students that process papers can have a purpose beyond the simple spreading of "how-to-do-it" information. Students will frequently become involved in a debate over Mitford's belief that this "prettying up" of the dead is excessive and absurd, with some arguing that the elaborate funeral ritual is essential for the living and others attacking it as sham. Such a debate might lead some students to investigate the legal burial requirements in their state and then to write an essay about their findings. And while many students find this essay distasteful, most agree that Mitford has performed a valuable service by publicizing the process so that people have enough information to make a choice regarding their own funeral or that of relatives. This essay provides an excellent opportunity to discuss use of vivid, sensory details and their effects on the reader. Mitford's carefully selected word choice ("the embalmer . . . returns to the attack") should be analyzed as the class discusses the essay's tone. This essay may also be used to introduce such terms as euphemism and personification; whereas Mitford's easily recognized transition devices might emphasize a lesson on coherence.

Answers to Questions, p. 210

1. Mitford feels that, in contrast to earlier days, Americans are now paying millions for a process they know nothing about. The reason is not the gruesomeness of the subject nor Americans' lack of curiosity, but the almost universal desire of undertakers to keep the process a secret. Mitford implies that if people did understand the embalming process, they might begin to question whether they wanted or needed such a service. Her attitude toward the morticians is critical; she obviously believes that people should have access to information on the embalming process.

2. Yes. There are numerous examples of descriptions that appeal to the senses. Below are listed only a few:

    Sight: "Positioning the lips is a problem. The lips should give the impression of being ever so slightly parted. . . . Up drift can sometimes be remedied by pushing one or two straight pins through the inner margin of the lower lip and then inserting them between the two front upper teeth" (paragraph 9).

Smell: "About three to six gallons of a dyed and perfumed solution of formaldehyde, glycerin, borax, phenol, alcohol and water is soon circulating through Mr. Jones . . ." (paragraph 9).

Touch: "If Flextone is used . . . the skin retains a velvety softness, the tissues are rubbery and pliable" (paragraph 8).

3. Mitford wants her readers to identify and sympathize with the corpse, to understand that the body suffering such indignities was once a living person.

4. Mitford feels that this process is unnecessary, expensive, and degrading. Her tone may be described as ironic or sarcastic. To "have at" him makes Mr. Jones seem like a piece of meat, as does "returning to the attack in the next example." Friends will say ". . . exposes the fake piety of those who aren't really close to the deceased and can only comment on the embalmer's skill. The caution about the placement of the body mocks the undertaker's inappropriate elevation of a trivial concern." In the context of grieving survivors, and the sarcastic: "Here he will hold open house . . ." makes it sound like he is still alive.

5. She quotes the undertakers and textbooks to show the funeral business's crass and depersonalized treatment of the dead. They seem preoccupied with the need to artificially "beautify" the body, regardless of the means (kitchen cleanser and nail polish on the teeth, pins in the lips, wire through the jaw, etc.). The dead person becomes little more than a department store dummy to be dressed for some sort of freak fashion show. Mitford quotes the undertakers themselves to show the readers that the callous descriptions are not her words but theirs. The quote in paragraph 7 says that even though research on embalming is "haphazard," undertakers are advised (for "best results") to begin embalming before life is "completely extinct," that is, before all the body's cells are dead. Mitford implies that undertakers might be so eager to achieve those best results that they might begin too soon; but she ironically concludes that at least there is no risk of accidentally burying anyone alive: after all, embalming removes the blood.

6. Mitford quotes euphemisms such as "Repose Block" and "Slumber Room" to show how the funeral business tries to sugarcoat death for the living by pretending the dead person is only asleep or resting. Terms such as "dermasurgeon" are used to give embalmers more prestige by linking their work to that of physicians, especially plastic surgeons.

7. The words in paragraph 10 connote a defenseless person being attacked by the mortician. The series of questions in paragraph 12 reproduces the flippant tone Mitford thinks characterizes the embalmer's attitude toward the bodies. The corpse is not a dead person worthy of respect but merely a challenge to the embalmer's ingenuity. One can almost hear Mitford's sarcastic imitation of a mortician saying, "Head off? Hey, no problem."

8. Yes. Beginning with paragraph 4: "first" (paragraphs 3–4); "preparation room" (4–5); "first," "embalming" (5–6); "another" (6–7); "to return to" (7–8); "soon," "Mr. Jones" (8–9); "The next step" (9–10); "all this attention" (10–11); "returns" (11–12); "The opposite condition" (12–13); parallel construction of "If Mr. Jones . . ." (14–15); "completed," "now" (15–16); "now ready" (16–17); "next" (17–18).

9. Yes. The idea of a corpse holding "open house" for visitors is ridiculous. But ridiculous, according to Mitford, is the correct term for what embalmers try to do: dress up and beautify a dead body as if it were hosting a party.

10. Some students may argue that the funeral business makes it easier for the living to accept the death of a friend or relative and that this comfort justifies the artificial "dandifying" of the body. Others may agree with Mitford, adding that the cost of funerals today is also unreasonable.

Vocabulary

1. docility (1)—meekness, obedience
2. perpetuation (1)—continuance
3. inherent (2)—basic, intrinsic
4. mandatory (2)—obligatory
5. intractable (3)—obstinate, not easily governed or controlled
6. reticence (3)—reluctance
7. raison d'être (3)—French for "reason to be"
8. ingenious (5)—brilliant
9. cadaver (5)—a dead body
10. somatic (7)—pertaining to, or affecting, the body
11. rudimentary (7)—basic, elementary
12. dispel (7)—remove
13. pliable (8)—easily bent, supple
14. semblance (11)—form or outward appearance
15. ravages (11)—violently destructive effects
16. stippling (12)—painting by means of dots or small spots
17. emaciation (13)—wasted or depleted condition

2A. Process Analysis: Directional

"Preparing for the Job Interview: Know Thyself" by Katy Piotrowski—p. 212

Discussion
Piotrowski's essay is a brief but thorough step-by-step analysis of how to prepare for a job interview.

Answers to Questions, p. 213

1. The process described prepares job candidates by giving them the steps to follow to prepare and present themselves for an interview.
2. The author gives step-by-step directions on how to proceed from preparation through the end of the interview.
3. The following are the steps involved in preparing for the interview:
   1) identify three responsibilities of the job;
   2) describe at least three examples from your past that demonstrate expertise in those areas and think of other experiences in your professional life that might show you as a viable candidate—describe the situation or tasks, talk about the actions you took, finish with the results of your efforts, and frame your answers using action verbs that show leadership;
   3) prepare and practice general information about your work history highlights, education, and why you are excited about the job;

4) investigate the company to which you are applying—its goals, products, services, and recent publicity;

5) think about questions you can ask the employer; and

6) thank the interviewer(s) for their time.

4. The organizational structure follows the steps in the order they should be taken. By using Shawn to explain the process, readers have some idea of where they, themselves, might stumble. She also allows the speaker to further explore and explain.

5. Piotrowski's examples further our understanding of what she means by certain terms. They also provide choices, as in paragraph 6, of ideas that might otherwise be difficult to narrow down.

6. "First" (2), "moving on" (3), "in addition to" (4), "As well as" (5) are some paragraph openers that help transition. The author also uses content, for example, staying on the topic of questions at the end of paragraph 5 and beginning of paragraph 6.

7. Her only warning is not to forget to thank the interviewers, but in a larger way she is warning candidates to be prepared.

8. In paragraph three, Piotrowski numbers the steps of the subprocess and gives it the acronym, STAR, to distinguish it from the larger process.

9. Her tone is friendly and professional. It is appropriate and effective for she allows us to participate in a professional experience and eases the tension for us. She begins with her narrative, which invites us into the conversation. Responses will vary on the specifics.

10. The conclusion helps to frame the essay by returning our attention to Shawn and revealing that she got the job, thus showing the reader that the methods he or she just learned actually work.

Vocabulary

1. expertise (2)—extensive knowledge and experience
2. implemented (3)—conducted or installed, coordinated
3. prospective (5)—potential, viable

3. Comparison and Contrast: Point-by-Point Pattern

"Grant and Lee: A Study in Contrasts" by Bruce Catton—p. 227

Discussion

This is one of the most famous (and most frequently anthologized) essays that students will come across. The author is well known for his encyclopedic knowledge of and writings about the Civil War, and this excerpt reflects not only that knowledge but also Catton's empathy for the period and many of the principal characters of that tragic conflict. It is also a concrete example of the three ways to avoid what Wyrick calls the "so what?" thesis. The subject has a universal appeal—it demonstrates something about principled soldiers in a native American conflict that can apply to us all, even if we are not in a "war," but merely in an argument. It is directed to Americans interested in a vital part of our history, and it especially shows "a particular relationship between two subjects." The major method of organization—contrast—announces itself in the title, and the development is essentially by the "point-by-point" method. There is, however, some comparison at the end that provides not only some perspective, but an effective conclusion as well.

Answers to Questions, p. 230

1. The thesis is contained in all of paragraph 3.

2. A good summary of Lee's view of society is in paragraph 5, where Catton states that Lee represented "the age of chivalry transplanted to a New World." The old idea of the Great Chain of Being is a good analogy to Lee's social ideal. Some were higher on the chain than others, but those higher up needed to see their favored position not as a justification for abusing those lower down, but as a position of responsibility from which they had the means and the power to improve society as a whole and not just their own lot in life. Catton describes Lee in terms that might also be applied to, say, the men of the Kennedy dynasty: the quintessential man of leisure whose concern for his version of society makes him not only a great defender of a humanitarian aristocracy, but an even greater symbol of what the South stood for and what Confederate soldiers were fighting for.

3. Catton describes Grant as both the product and the embodiment of the pioneers and the pioneer spirit. These people looked at the social structure of the country as virtually non-existent, except as it promoted and defended the principle that society serves the individual, not the other way around. It was the rugged individuals who tamed the land west of the mountains, fought uncountable odds to survive, and forged a democracy from their labors. "As [the Nation's] horizons expanded, so did [the individual's]," and everyone could be anything they wished, uninhibited by class or other social restrictions. It was the raucous vitality of those stimulated by the newness of the land and the society, not the reasoned judgments of those representing the old social class of the landed gentry, that gave America its spirit and energy.

4. Catton uses the point-by-point pattern to develop his essay in paragraphs 4–16, contrasting the generals' backgrounds, philosophies, and the views they embodied as well as comparing their shared personal traits.

5. Catton begins to compare the greatness in each man—the fact that they were both great fighters, had enormous tenacity, were daring and resourceful, and could turn quickly from war to peace.

6. Within paragraphs, Catton tends to move from general to specific, to set up a background or milieu, and then place one general and then the other within it as an outgrowth of his particular background or social circumstance. For example, "Lee was tidewater Virginia. . . . A land that was beginning all over again . . . In such a land . . . was . . . [a] class of men who lived not to gain advantage for themselves . . . [and] Lee embodied the noblest elements of this aristocratic ideal." Catton not only varies the sentence structure and length to avoid choppiness, he even uses sentence structure to emphasize a point, like the short "individual" sentences in paragraph 8 that are not woven together as tightly as in other paragraphs and thereby "compete" on their own for attention, much like people did on the frontier. Between paragraphs, Catton uses transition words like "yet" and "lastly" as well as repeating words and phrases from previous material. Paragraph 7, for example, begins "Grant . . . was everything Lee was not."

7. As befits his status as one of our best writers, Catton states his intentions in topic sentences and then delivers what he promises. In paragraph 8, for example, the topic is how the frontier men were opposites of the tidewater aristocrats. Each sentence in the paragraph is unified coherently around the topic, and each has its own minicontrast around that point. In paragraph 5, each sentence is devoted to describing in ever more detail the

tidewater Virginia background of Lee. Catton could perhaps be faulted for not including enough concrete detail, going no further than abstractions like "solemn obligations" or "self-reliant to a fault," but overall, there seems to be enough detail to make the points of contrast between the two men.

8. The advantage of the single sentence in paragraph 3 is that it isolates the thesis and provides a break from the introductory material in paragraph 2. Paragraph 4 is like a headline announcing the beginning of the contrast as well as the key element of the description of both men—an old aristocracy in a new world. In Lee's case, Catton shows how Lee embodied this aristocracy; in Grant's case, Catton highlights how different Grant was from that old aristocratic notion.

9. Catton has a high opinion of both, and the tone is admiring but not fawning. This tone creates an atmosphere that is neither frivolous nor hostile to one side, reflecting, again, Catton's balanced admiration for both of these great Americans. The aristocratic South, always easy to criticize as not conducive to democratic ideals and structures, is portrayed by Catton as populated by people meeting "solemn obligations" and looking to its leadership "to give it strength and virtue." Similarly, the individual pioneer was not merely a competitive animal, but one who had a "deep sense of belonging to a national community." The tone of the essay, therefore, comes across as neither argumentative nor merely informative, nor aggressively jingoistic but appropriately serious, thoughtful, and (most important) empathetic to both men who have come to represent two significant regions of the United States.

10. The comparison of both men turning quickly from war to peace suggests the end of the war, the end of their roles as generals, and their final meeting as a paradigm of what the relationship between the North and the South should now be. The end of the essay suggests the scene at the beginning, and as this moment in history ends, so does the essay.

Vocabulary

1. chivalry (5)—social behavior reflecting that idealized by medieval knights, i.e., politeness, honor, self-sacrifice
2. deportment (5)—body language, behavior
3. embodied (6)—an abstraction made concrete
4. tenacity (11)—the quality of holding on for a long time
5. diametrically (12)—totally opposite
6. burgeoning (12)—growing, ballooning
7. indomitable (14)—unbeatable, unable to be dominated
8. reconciliation (16)—the settlement or resolution of a dispute

3A. Comparison and Contrast: Block Method

"Two Ways of Viewing the River" by Samuel Clemens—p. 231

Discussion

While many students will have read the novels of Samuel Clemens (Mark Twain), few of them may be familiar with his essays. "Two Ways of Viewing the River" is an intriguing piece for class discussion since rather than contrasting two different subjects, as is most often done (see "Grant and Lee: A Study in Contrasts"), Clemens presents two vastly different perspectives of the same subject. It might be emphasized that the actual features of the river remain the same (the sunset, the floating log); it is Clemens's vision of the river that has changed. Students might be asked to complete a timed, in-class freewriting exercise in which they contrast two very different perspectives they have had of one unchanging subject. For example, they might contrast their first impression with a later view of someone they now know well. Discussion of these student writings could reveal the importance of descriptive detail in comparison/contrast essays.

Answers to Questions, p. 232

1. Clemens is contrasting his personal, emotional view of the river when he was new to steamboating with his later view as a captain. His thesis is embodied in the first three sentences: While a captain's perspective is valuable and gives a sense of accomplishment, it has sadly replaced an earlier, mystical connection to the river.

2. Clemens chooses the block method of development. One reason this choice is appropriate is because he can contrast the same observations (e.g., the floating log, the tall dead tree) in each block; a reader would not get lost in the points of contrast from block to block. A more significant reason that this is not only an appropriate choice, but also may be the best choice for this selection is that the first block sets a mood in its totality that is necessary to understand before the reader can understand the loss implied in the more sterile and cold second block.

3. The second sentence in paragraph 2 provides a transition for the reader. Clemens moves the reader ahead in time to a later view of the river "when I began to cease from noting the glories and the charms which the moon and the sun and the twilight wrought upon the river's face."

4. Clemens's reference to doctors in the final paragraph broadens the meaning of this excerpt. Not only was this an experience in his life, but he also suggests that the understanding might extend to a more universal experience.

5. The questions encourage the reader to think about a more universal application of Clemens's experience. The last question asks the reader to think further: Is the loss of innocent wonder and splendor worth the gain of accomplishment and professionalism?

6. The language in paragraph 1 is rich, lush, sensual, and poetic. The diction appropriately creates the mood of wonder and magnificence for the reader to contrast to the more businesslike language of the second view.

7. These similes provide a more visual image for the reader: ". . . as many-tinted as an opal . . ." ". . . trail that shone like silver."

8. The language in paragraph 2 is more sparse and pictureless. The visions and feelings relative to the river are unimportant; only the usefulness of the objects and the dangers created by them are important to a good captain.

9. Clemens personifies the "new snag" when he claims it will "fish for steamboats." This personification adds a certain element of alienation and antagonism to his later view of the river, which contrasts sharply with his earlier perspective.

10. While the mood of each contrasting block is distinctly different—the earlier block is warm and sensual while the latter is harsh and professional—the tone of the entire essay is rather consistent. Throughout the selection, Clemens has a sense of nostalgia and reflection over times and feelings gone by.

Vocabulary

1. trifling (1)—being of small value or importance
2. acquisition (1)—something gained
3. conspicuous (1)—easy to see; attracting attention
4. ruddy (1)—reddish; glowing
5. wrought (2)—fashioned or made, usually with great care
6. compassing (3)—providing direction for

4. Definition

"The Munchausen Mystery" by Don R. Lipsitt—p. 245

Discussion

Discussing the clarity with which Lipsitt defines this complex syndrome for a lay reader provides the opportunity to discuss the importance of audience considerations in a definition essay. What words and techniques indicate the targeted audience? Students might research a professional definition of this disease (or *hypochondria*) and compare the two. What are the different purposes? While the reason writers define terms and concepts for lay audiences is rather obvious, professional definitions are necessary for other reasons. Why would a writer define a term for his or her peers? After discussing terms and concepts on which students are the experts, they might practice writing two definitions of one of these terms, one for someone at a similar level as themselves and one for a novice reader.

Answers to Questions, p. 247

1. The example illustrates the syndrome that Lipsitt will define. A reader will immediately see the intriguing—mystifying—nature of this strange condition.
2. The title indicates a strangeness and puzzling quality to this disease, which makes for much more reader interest than a title that would merely suggest a practical definition.
3. Because of the large number of Munchausen patients, the condition accounts for enormous expenses for the health-care system, expenses that are usually not reimbursed.
4. Knowing the origin of the name increases the reader's understanding of the fictional nature of the condition and the wandering of the patient from one medical provider to the next. Also, the unusual name might leave a lingering question in the reader's mind if it were not addressed.
5. Without the specific examples, a reader could hardly imagine the extremes to which a patient goes to feign illness.
6. The specific patients illustrate the extent to which these individuals persist in their charades. Students might believe an extended example of one particular patient might be even more interesting and instructive.
7. By contrasting Munchausen to hypochondria, Lipsitt refines the definition more distinctly. Munchausen involves not only false illness, but intentional, conscious deception.
8. When Lipsitt explains the causes of Munchausen, he anticipates a typical reader's question, as most would wonder why anyone would try so compulsively to deceive physicians. Also, a full (extended) definition of any disease should include its causes in order to understand its progression.

9. The conclusion is effective because it acknowledges what little is known (and has been explained in the definition) about the syndrome while suggesting there is yet more to learn before its occurrence can be reduced. This conclusion aligns to the author's extended definition.

10. Student responses will vary.

Vocabulary

1. fabricates (1)—makes up
2. mimic (2)—imitate
3. incurs (2)—meets with
4. hypochondriacs (4)—persons who believe they are ill
5. sputum (4)—saliva, spit
6. palpably (4)—obviously, easily perceived
7. feasible (4)—reasonable, workable
8. psychoanalytic (7)—pertaining to a method of treating mental disorders by analysis
9. paradoxically (7)—in a seemingly impossible manner
10. odyssey (9)—a long and complicated journey

5. Division and Classification: Classification

"The Plot against People" by Russell Baker—p. 256

Discussion

As Baker's essay is comic in tone and his purpose is to entertain, class discussion of humor writing is valid here, particularly as many freshman composition students will want to try their hand at comic writing at some point in the course. Ask students if the 1968 publication date limits the effectiveness of Baker's essay in present day. Is it dated in any way? If so, what parts of the essay are dated, and which still seem fresh and effective? Note the importance of word choice. For example, Baker consistently refers to "man" and "mankind." Would this language be considered sexist today? If they were to update Baker's essay, what changes would student writers make? Why?

Answers to Questions, p. 258

1. Baker's purpose is to entertain his audience by presenting humorous truisms they are likely to empathize with and understand.

2. The thesis statement is the opening sentence of his essay. While students might argue that a more fully developed lead-in would be effective, it should be noted that Baker's direct statement of focus has an appeal of its own as it cuts directly to the essay's subject and provokes the thoughts of the reader.

3. Baker's categories for inanimate objects include "those that don't work, those that break down and those that get lost." He classifies these objects according to behavior—"The method each object uses to achieve its purpose," which is to "resist" and "ultimately defeat" mankind.

4. Baker gives examples to illustrate each category fully and to allow his audience to empathize; readers will recognize the purse that disappears, the furnace that breaks down, and the flashlight that never works. The specifics are a strength of Baker's essay.

5. The category "those that break down" is particularly well developed. Students might cite the example of the automobile (paragraphs 2, 3, and 4). Or, if students argue that "those that get lost" is particularly vivid, the example of the lost purse might be mentioned (paragraphs 8 and 10).

6. Some examples of personification in the essay include the automobile "with the cunning typical of its breed," the notion that appliances are "in league" to cause maximum frustration for humans, and the idea that "those that don't work" "have truly defeated man by conditioning him never to expect anything of them." This personification is a key part of Baker's humor.

7. Baker's mock-scientific word choice is important to the essay's success (e.g., "Some persons believe this constitutes evidence that inanimate objects are not entirely hostile to man"). A serious essay on this subject is likely to fail because of lack of purpose. Would anyone actually enjoy a factual essay that notes that purses do, indeed, get lost, and automobiles do, in fact, break down?

8. The essay's title reveals the common link between the categories as Baker establishes his "us versus them" comic note.

9. One way to change Baker's language for gender concerns is to use plural nouns and pronouns in lieu of references to "man" and any male pronouns. For example in paragraph two, instead of "man" we can use "people" and instead of "him" we can use "us." In paragraph 7 we can delete "no man" and use "no one," whereas deleting "to man" in paragraph 11 still maintains the sense of the sentence, and replacing "a man" with "some" will also suffice. In paragraph 16, "us" and "we" will work, whereas we need to use a possessive in 17, such as "our."

10. Student responses will vary. Instructors might note that Baker is breaking the traditional composition rule that mandates a minimum of two sentences in a paragraph. The stark finality of Baker's one-sentence conclusion increases the impact of his parting message.

Vocabulary

1. inanimate (1)—lifeless, inorganic
2. cunning (3)—craftiness, slyness
3. evolve (6)—develop, unfold, produce
4. locomotion (7)—movement
5. virtually (9)—practically
6. inherent (10)—essential, innate
7. constitutes (11)—forms, establishes, sets up
8. conciliatory (12)—appeasing, forgiving
9. barometer (13)—instrument that measures atmospheric pressure and helps weather prediction

5A. Division and Classifications: Division

"A Brush with Reality: Surprises in the Tube" by David Bodanis—p. 259

Discussion

Bodanis writes an essay of division on the topic of toothpaste ingredients. He does so with wit and wisdom, breaking down the parts into categories of large and small particles, and offensive and dangerous elements. His language is both scientific and casual as he first identifies the ingredients formally and then explains them using everyday language and clarifying examples and comparisons.

Answers to Questions, p. 261

1. The essay displays division by breaking the whole into parts, by looking at the distinct ingredients of toothpaste.
2. Bodanis intends to inform readers that they unnecessarily ingest potentially harmful ingredients each morning through what seems a harmless and necessary product. He wants readers to be repulsed and stop using toothpaste.
3. The parts are arranged according to two principles: from the largest particles to the smallest and then from the least offensive and dangerous to the most so.
4. Bodanis describes the ingredients using both their technical and layman's terms, indicating that his audience is general—the consumer.
5. Bodanis is fairly thorough, right down to the germs in the bathroom. He does, however, neglect the packaging and its impact on the product.
6. By mentioning an ingredient's use in other products, Bodanis both makes a comparison that allows a broader perception and, at the same time, influences a negative reaction by comparing it to something that one would not put in one's mouth.
7. As noted above, Bodanis compares ingredients to noxious elements intended to repel readers. Using cause and effect, he shows how an ingredient actually does the job it is intended to do, but when we understand this aspect, we are forced to consider the possible long-term effects, such as large dental bills or perhaps the loss of our teeth altogether. Anyone who knows anything about dentistry will tell you that pits in the teeth attract decay and so while this may seem to be a slippery slope, it is not.
8. Responses will vary but such things as "a large helping of gummy molecules" (8), "seaweed ooze" (8), and "big gobs" (2) suggest a reckless accounting in the recipe and liven the piece. His sarcasm in such statements as "Only two major chemicals are left to make the refreshing, cleansing substance we know as toothpaste," (9) and "whipped in with the rest of the toothpaste the manufacturers can sell it at a neat and accountant-pleasing $2 per pound equivalent" (2) reveals his attitude toward the manufacturing companies.
9. In paragraph 9, Bodanis is recapping the ingredients to remind us where we are in the list. Here, too, he is dividing the ingredients into subcategories—the first involves cleansers. In paragraph 12, the category is disinfectants, and in 13 the entire list is recapped and amended with fluoride to contrast a simpler substitute ingredient—water, which is the main ingredient in toothpaste and the one with which he began.
10. Responses will vary, yet it should be noted that his final sentence demonstrates a simple honesty that mimics the simple ingredient of water and thus has a stronger impact than a more convoluted conclusion.

Vocabulary

1. splayed (1)—spread out
2. extruded (1)—pressed out, squeezed out as through a tube
3. lucrative (2)—financially worthwhile
4. aeons (4)—indefinitely long time, longer than an era

5. abrading (4)—the act of rubbing away with a sharp tool such as sandpaper
6. carnage (5)—the dead remains of men or animals, slaughter, massacre
7. cavernous (5)—extremely large and cavelike
8. errant (5)—stray or straying from the norm or the expected
9. gustatory (11)—associated with the sense of taste
10. intrudant (12)—one that enters uninvited

6. Causal Analysis

"Some Lessons from the Assembly Line" by Andrew Braaksma—p. 271

Discussion

Braaksma's essay is a lesson in the realities of blue-collar work. He claims that working on an assembly line in a factory during the summer months away from school, rather than taking on easier part-time work, has given him a clearer perspective of what his life would have been like if he hadn't gone to college and then what his college education really means to his future.

Answers to Questions, p. 273

1. The reason he appreciates school is because he works summers in a factory and he finds the work harder than schoolwork. The essay focuses on the causes of his relief and his belief in school while describing the long hours, physical demands, insecurity, and feeble pay of blue-collar work.
2. He has learned how lucky he is to get an education, how to work hard, how easy it is to lose work, and he is inspired to make the most of college before entering the "real" world.
3. He begins with a brief narrative that then compares and contrasts his school environment to his work environment. He continues to contrast his expectations to his reality, his job to other students' jobs and his perspective to theirs, his long hours to his pay check, his own future reality to that of his coworkers, his luck to those without it, his laziness at school to his hard work at the factory, and his time on the line to that of his coworkers.
4. "Stamping, cutting, welding, moving, assembling" are some of the verbs that reveal his work. He also mentions work beginning at 6:00 a. m., an environment of "hulking, spark-showering machines," and "schedules and quotas" that are "rigid."
5. Paragraph one details the sights and sounds of the factory, whereas two describes his work. Paragraph four compares hours to pay and details problems with machinery and employers. Paragraph five reveals his expectation to go to college and his reality there of skipping classes and turning in lazy work, while paragraph six reveals reactions of coworkers to his textbooks.
6. He does this to show the meaning of real work—that it is hard and can't be abused in the way schoolwork can. Some readers will be offended, but most will probably nod in agreement. He values the hard work he has learned to perform, despite his desire to avoid it in the future.
7. His sense of guilt comes from knowing that he is taking a job from someone who may need it and doesn't have the means to go to college. Moreover, he has the opportunity to escape the oppression of factory work every fall and spring, while others will toil away their whole lives.

8. The dialogue here helps to make his coworkers real to the reader. It also adds a perspective that helps support Braaksma's sense of guilt and his understanding that it isn't just he who finds the work hard.

9. He begins with the French literature class that he notes is a long way from factory life, so that when he returns to the class in the end he is referencing the quality of life he leads as a student and appreciating his new understanding that he came to learn the hard way.

10. Responses will vary.

Vocabulary

1. blue-collar (2)—reference to workers who toil with their hands in factories, as opposed to white-collar work that relates to those who wear white shirts and push pencils

2. lush (2)—full of botanical greenery

3. cavernous (2)—large, deep, and dark as a cave

4. cocksure (4)—arrogant

5. downsizing (4)—a term used by big business to indicate layoffs and cutbacks

6. tinged (6)—tainted, hued, or suggesting a color, feeling, or idea

7. voyeuristic (6)—having a sense of watching others without them knowing

8. discreetly (6)—quietly or politely, tactfully or judiciously

Chapter **10**

Argumentation
p. 277

■ **Summary**

Developing Your Essay

- choose an appropriate title
- explore possibilities and your opinions
- anticipate opposing views
- know and remember your audience
- decide which points of argument to include
- organize clearly (patterns A, B, C, and combination)
- argue logically (by example, comparison/contrast, cause/effect, definition)
- offer evidence to support claims (personal experience, testimony, facts, statistics, etc.)
- find appropriate tone
- consider Rogerian techniques if appropriate

Problems to Avoid

Common Logical Fallacies

- hasty generalizations
- *non sequitur*
- begging the question
- red herring
- *post hoc, ergo propter hoc*
- *ad hominem*
- faulty use of authority
- *ad populum*
- circular thinking
- either/or
- hypostatization
- bandwagon appeal
- straw man
- faulty analogy
- quick fix

Practicing What You've Learned, p. 289

Assignment

Essay Topics

A Topic Proposal for Your Essay

- identify the subject of your argument and write a rough opinion statement
- state at least one reason for choosing this topic
- identify your audience and purpose
- list at least two reasons that support your opinion
- clearly state at least one opposing opinion
- identify any difficulties that might arise during drafting

Sample Student Essay

Professional Essays

Questions on Content, Structure, and Style, p. 298

Analyzing Advertisements

- Conflicting Positions: Gun Control
- Competing Products: Sources of Energy
- Popular Appeals: Spending Our Money

A Revision Worksheet

Reviewing Your Progress

■ Answers to "Practicing What You've Learned" Exercises

Practicing What You've Learned, p. 289

A. Numbers 1, 6, 7, 9, 10, and 13 argue for allowing home schoolers to play. Numbers 2, 3, 4, 5, 8, 9, 11, and 12 argue against allowing home schoolers to play. Number 8 presents an option for logical argument.

B. "Ban Those Books"

Paragraph 1:

- argument *ad populum* (use of scare tactics: "very existence . . . is threatened")
- either/or fallacy ("cleanse or reconcile ourselves")

Paragraph 2:

- hypostatization ("History has shown")
- begging the question ("immoral books," "Communist plot")
- argument *ad hominem* ("liberal free-thinkers and radicals" are threatening names to some people)
- *post hoc* (the number of cut classes and the decline in the number of seniors going on to college were not necessarily caused by placing the books in the library that year)

Paragraph 3:

- either/or fallacy ("natural decline . . . or the influence of those dirty books")
- *non sequitur* (obviously, other reasons can exist for the changes in the students' behavior)
- begging the question ("dirty books," "undesirable characters")
- argument *ad populum* ("innocent children")

Paragraph 4:

- argument *ad populum* ("simple man . . . farm boy" versus the "pseudointellectuals," "Communist conspiracy," "good folks")
- bandwagon appeal (all the "right-thinking neighbors")

USA Today: "High Schools, Wake Up!" and Paul D. Houston's Opposing View, "Reform No Child's Play" —p. 296

Discussion

These two essays debate the value of changing the schedule for high school students to a later hour to accommodate for research findings that teens require more sleep than they get in order to function normally.

Answers to Questions, p. 298

1. *USA Today* editors believe changing the school schedule is a good idea.

2. Keeping earlier start times for teens works well for sports coaches, employers and employees, and work-bound parents. It does not work well for teens because they usually stay up later than small children, causing them to be sleep deprived. As a result they nod off in class, are grouchy and poorer learners, and are more prone to attention deficit disorders and cutting classes.

3. The named universities have sleep research centers that report findings supporting the editorial board's position.

4. The results of moving start times forward for teens include better school attendance and grades, happier students, and safer teens.

5. The objections the author mentions relate to school bus schedules and money, teens earn in after-school jobs. He only deals with the bus scheduling and offers a solution.

6. These schools successfully changed start times.

7. The major objections Houston offers are these: younger children standing in the dark at bus stops, local industries and businesses losing student labor, parents not able to get to work as early, and some state dictates as to school calendars. He would do well to name the specific states and discuss the details in each objection.

8. Answers will vary, but students should see it as an opening that presents the opposing argument's basis for changing start times. As such he is framing his argument around the issue he wants to begin with. He does not deal with it as such in his discussion.

9. Answers will vary here as well. *USA Today's* conclusion, however, should be seen as the stronger of the two. It has a clear, definitive position reiterated and supported. Houston's conclusion is weak in that he leaves the issue as one that needs more discussion.

10. Again, answers will vary. Areas to consider for revision in Houston's article involve citing sources. He should consider revamping the focus toward the educational issues or more closely connecting the ideas he has in terms of benefits to students and then to the larger community. Moreover, while both articles would benefit from more specific details—*USA Today's* in the form of the impact on the community—Houston needs to rethink his overall purpose as well.

Suggestions for Writing

Vocabulary

USA Today essay:

1. aka (1)—abbreviation of "also known as"
2. scarfed (1)—ate quickly
3. grouchier (3)—more ill tempered than usual or most
4. prone (3)—have a tendency toward something
5. shortsighted (7)—near sighted or not thinking far enough into the future
6. status quo (8)—what the current level of operation is

Houston's essay:

1. folklore (1)—beliefs based on stories of experience
2. unique (1)—one of a kind
3. systemic (2)—occurring within a system and self perpetuating
4. confound (2)—to make confusing or difficult to comprehend or complete
5. implement (5)—to begin on a course of action or to initiate an idea

■ Discussion, Answers to Questions, Vocabulary

Analyzing Advertisements, p. 299

Conflicting Positions: Gun Control

Student responses to these advertisements will vary. Instructors might use discussion of these advertisements to emphasize that one's personal beliefs about gun control and the safe use of energy should not make the reader blind to the various appeals—both effective and flawed—that the advertisements employ. Some of the appeals used are listed below.

N.R.A. advertisement gives biographical details that present Gutman as a successful business and civic leader and family-oriented man: emphasizes his experiences in communist Cuba and the Florida legislature to add authority to his support for the N.R.A., thus perhaps strengthening the credibility of the N.R.A. for the reader.

Center to Prevent Handgun Violence advertisement: emphasizes the contrast between "self-styled 'citizen militias'" that cite the Second Amendment as support for their weapons and military training, and the National Guard, which the ad states is the true militia protected by the Second Amendment (the photo of the militia group plays on reader emotions); Supreme Court justice Warren Burger's views are quoted (appealing to reader's regard for intellectual authority) to strengthen the advertisement's claim that the Second Amendment does not prohibit gun-control laws.

The Right to Bears and Arms advertisement: emphasizes the number of deaths associated with guns while suggesting that guns have fewer manufacturing regulations than teddy bears. Appeals largely to emotions centered on children and implicates gun manufacturers heavily in the accidental deaths of children.

Competing Products: Sources of Energy, p. 303

Discussion

In these three ads, students will have various responses to the visual appeals and effectiveness, but the arguments can be viewed as fairly straightforward.

Metropolitan Energy Council, Inc. advertisement: the emotional appeals here are to fear and protection of loved ones, especially children—an ad populum argument for parents (a mother and her toddler are pictured) that focuses on the danger of gas heat, a belief that is based on no concrete evidence (at least in the ad). The ad also insinuates that because the gas companies are large, they are also impersonal, a non sequitur, and because of this they don't care about their customers and are therefore negligent. This is a red herring and has no basis in fact.

Xcel Energy advertisement: this ad tries to educate the consumer about gas smells and what to do in case of a leak. It also appeals to intellect and to protection of loved ones, but in this case the latter is a direct response to the concerns in the previous ad. Running an ad that appears to be a public safety announcement makes the company appear caring and concerned for the welfare of the public, much in the way parents would be for their children.

U.S. Council for Energy Awareness advertisement: a largely emotional appeal centered on the photo of a baby sea turtle. It emphasizes the environmental safety of nuclear energy by implying that it has less negative impact on endangered species and fragile ecosystems than other energy sources. This ad argues against oil and gas as pollutants. It appeals to protection of children and the environment via the baby turtle, but it begs the question of whether or not nuclear energy is safe.

PETA: The PETA ad equates fur to pets and relies on the fact that most pet owners regard their pets as friends that they wouldn't think of hurting. The initial comparison of fur to an animal requires that the fur not be thought of as separate from the animal and assumes (begs the questions) that a skinned animal will be harmed in the process of taking its fur. Oddly, no one seems to consider this a problem when shearing sheep for wool, which is probably what Charlize Theron's lovely shawl is made from.

Popular Appeals: Spending Our Money, p. 307

Discussion

Who doesn't eat peanut butter sandwiches? In the American Century ad, the idea of the peanut butter sandwich as an icon of American lunchboxes stands out as a "bandwagon appeal." Here the company identity is down home, responsible, reliable, hard-working. An investment service must generate trust and this ad appeals to simple folk needing simple, clear investment advice from a trustworthy company.

Well, if Pierce Brosnan, otherwise known as James Bond, wears the Omega watch, then we should all wear one. The bandwagon appeal here is employed in the idea of everyone wanting to be like James Bond, so the effect is that if I buy one I can experience the thrill vicariously. The name "Seamaster Aqua Terra" enhances the consumer's connection to Bond toys such as his amphibious cars, and as such to a sense of fun, adventure, and power.

Chapter  11

Description

p. 313

■ Summary

How to Write Effective Description

- recognize your purpose
- describe clearly, using specific details—select only appropriate details
- make your descriptions vivid

Problems to Avoid

- remember your audience
- avoid an erratic organization of details—avoid any sudden change in perspective

Practicing What You've Learned, p. 318

A. In *The (Old) Buffalo Nickel,* Klinkenborg subjectively describes and compares the old buffalo nickel of 1913 and the newer one of 2005. Clearly the writer hopes to reveal that the old nickel is "iconographic" in its representation of the west before it was "tamed" by the government of the United States, and he bemoans its loss. The buffalo facing left on the old nickel would represent the west. That the "coin can barely contain the creature" is indicative of the impression that the buffalo was once a proud and plentiful beast that ruled the plains and ran with the Native Americans while providing them with food, pelts, tools and such for survival. Meanwhile the new nickel's buffalo faces right, toward the east, and is fenced in by the name of the country and thus implicitly by the country itself and serves little purpose now except as an attraction for those who visit places it still lives, like Yellowstone National Park and Custer State Park. Klinkenborg refers to a "tragic undertone of American history" in his final paragraph and in doing so makes clear his preference for the west facing bison's illumination of history.

B. Responses will vary.

Assignment

Essay Topics

A Topic Proposal for Your Essay

- identify your subject and whether you will describe it objectively or subjectively
- state at least one reason why you chose this topic
- identify your audience
- state your purpose and the effect you want to have on the reader
- list at least three details that will help clarify your subject
- identify difficulties that might arise during drafting

Sample Student Essay

Professional Essay

Questions on Content, Structure and Style, p. 328

Suggestions for Writing

Vocabulary

A Revision Worksheet

Reviewing Your Progress

■ Discussion, Answers to Questions, Vocabulary

"Still Learning from My Mother" by Cliff Schneider—p. 327

Discussion

Students might be encouraged to view this essay from a variety of perspectives, an idea that echoes Schneider's purpose as he brings in detail from a variety of memories and from comments made to him about his mother. This piece is reminiscent of the "my hero" or "my favorite role model" essay, but Schneider's details and focus draw the reader into this short description that invites the reader to glimpse life from multiple viewpoints of time, gender, values, and relationships.

Answers to Questions, p. 328

1. Text is primarily subjective as he describes his personal memories: "She never showed motherly concern, just a broad grin with the tip of her tongue exposed . . ." (1); "we'd notice this gleam in her eye" (2). Students will see others.

2. In 1950, most American mothers were housewives and homemakers whose primary domain was domestic, not athletic. Title IX called for education in athletics for all students, including women and thus changed the face of sports and women's lives dramatically in the latter half of the twentieth century. Prior to this amendment, however, while women did participate in athletics, very few were prominent in the public eye and fewer still would have participated in them in conjunction with their role as "mother."

3. The dominant impression Schneider leaves us with is of a woman who takes joy in athletic competition. Details provided are plentiful: "grabs a glove" (1); "lettered in field hockey . . . gleam in her eye . . . ready for action . . . to have some fun . . . played hard, laughed a lot . . ." (2); "protests [her 8-pound bowling ball] is too light and doesn't give enough pin action" (3); "This is the year I'm going to bowl a 200 game" (4); etc. Students will find such details throughout.

4. "She would happily grab a glove, run out to the road and then fire fast balls at me that cracked my glove . . ." (1); "She never showed motherly concern, just a broad grin with the tip of her tongue exposed . . ." (1); "we'd notice this gleam in her eye" (2). She has class because "win or lose, she was always gracious" (2).

5. The description appeals to the physical sensation in such a way that the reader can almost feel the sting. Sensory detail provides a physical response in the reader, not merely an intellectual nod of comprehension.

6. Her "perennial battle cry" reveals her as competitive, vivacious, goal oriented, and compelled to win, to achieve her best. Students may not be familiar with Vince Lombardi whose most famous quote is "Winning isn't everything; it's the only thing," which has been used to inspire male athletes and businessmen for the better part of a century.

7. Dialogue provides direct evidence of personality but where Schneider quotes a neighbor, he reveals a public perception of his mother that helps to support his own respect and reverence for her athletic ability. Such dialogue furthers his purpose for describing his mother's perseverance toward a goal.

8. The organization is chronological and allows the reader to view the character historically, showing her zest for competition and athleticism as part of her personality and not simply as a trendy adaptation or hobbylike recreation.

9. Schneider learns how to compete graciously, to play hard, to have fun, but mostly that he can still learn from her and that one is "never too old to dream and . . . to realize those dreams." The title of the essay helps to immediately establish Schneider's purpose. His goal is to show that learning needn't always be viewed in an educational setting and that it can be gained from unexpected sources. While we often consider mothers as teachers, in this case the stereotype is broken. This role reversal may provide a place to redirect discussion toward expectations in reading, biased thinking, or deconstruction of gender stereotypes. Reading this essay in conjunction with Heilbroner's in the following chapter will provide additional perspectives and writing opportunities for students.

10. Responses will vary.

Vocabulary

1. Title IX (2)—One of the Education Amendments of 1972—prohibited discrimination based on sex
2. diminished (3)—weakened; reduced
3. octogenarian (3)—a person in his or her 80s
4. concession (3)—something one concedes or gives up
5. toted (3)—carried
6. perennial (4)—returning seasonally; ongoing

C h a p t e r 12

Narration
p. 333

■ Summary

Extended Versus Brief Narratives

Writing the Effective Narrative Essay

- know your purpose
- make your main point clear
- follow a logical time sequence
- use sensory details to hold the reader's interest
- make your characters believable/authentic
- use dialogue realistically

Problems to Avoid

- choose your subject carefully
- limit your scope
- don't let your story lag with insignificant detail

Practicing What You've Learned, p. 336

Essay Topics

A Topic Proposal for Your Essay

- state the subject of your narrative
- state why you selected this narrative
- identify your audience
- identify your purpose, desired effect
- summarize in a few descriptive words the critical moment of your story
- identify potential difficulties in writing this narrative

Sample Student Essay

Professional Essay

Questions on Content, Structure, and Style, p. 345

Suggestions for Writing

Vocabulary

A Revision Worksheet

Reviewing Your Progress

■ Discussion, Answers to Questions, Vocabulary

"Sister Flowers" by Maya Angelou—p. 341

Discussion

Students might be encouraged to examine Angelou's narrative from two standpoints: her use of description, which allows her readers to see Sister Flowers and the essay's setting, and her use of dialogue, which allows her readers to hear key conversations. Why are both components necessary to present a fully rounded portrait of time, character, and place? A discussion of Angelou's use of specific and sensory details will enable students to examine ways to fully re-create scenes in their own narrative essays. Students may be interested to know that following the sexual abuse by her mother's husband, Angelou was mute for much of her childhood prior to meeting Mrs. Flowers.

Answers to Questions, p. 345

1. Angelou's main purpose is to show how Sister Flowers brought more than a love of language to her; Sister Flowers gave Angelou a sense of dignity and refinement she longed for.
2. The images Angelou uses to describe Sister Flowers set her apart from the rest of Stamps. The "private breeze" that surrounded her made her appear cool when the rest of the population was sweltering. In the description of Sister Flowers's appearance, the details again

set her apart, contrasting hers to the more typical farmer's appearance. Angelou's comparison of Sister Flowers's skin to the skin of a plum builds the image of delicacy and elegance. Although the reader knows Sister Flowers is "our side's answer to the richest white woman in town," Angelou tempers this image with a description of her genuine and warm smile.

3. Angelou sets up the reader for a later irony by having Momma speak to Sister Flowers in nonstandard English, by which Angelou is embarrassed. This early embarrassment is important because Sister Flowers makes a point of telling the young Angelou she should be tolerant of illiteracy.

4. As an adult, Angelou can see the relationship of mutual respect between her grandmother and Sister Flowers that reached across the educational differences.

5. Angelou was impressed by Mrs. Flowers because she was the closest thing in her culture to the elegant women in the literature Angelou read. She is compared to the heroines of novels. Angelou is glad never to have heard white people demean Sister Flowers because she would not want anything to tarnish this image of refinement and gentility.

6. Angelou was a very bright young girl who read constantly; the reader knows this from the many allusions to heroines of novels as well as the young Angelou's thoughts of *Beowulf* and *Oliver Twist*. Mrs. Flowers knows of her reading and also lets the reader know of Angelou's fine school work.

7. The extraordinary things about Sister Flowers's house—the ice on an ordinary day, white, fresh curtains, and a cookie plate covered with a tea towel—continued to set Mrs. Flowers apart from Angelou's existence. The cookies and lemonade were of crucial importance because they were made especially for Angelou and made her feel valued.

8. Dialogue is important to this section of the story because it is the sound of language that becomes so compelling to Angelou through Mrs. Flowers's reading. The words that Angelou utters after listening, spellbound, to Mrs. Flowers are the first she has uttered in a long time and they are more powerful in dialogue form.

9. Angelou's descriptive detail is complete and gives vivid pictures for the reader of places and people. Students may cite dialogue as important detail and also cite the vivid visual detail related to Mrs. Flowers and her home. Also, Angelou gives details of the feelings she was having throughout the experience. The reader understands her anxiety over what to wear, her attempt to use her best manners, her excitement over hearing the words of *A Tale of Two Cities* spoken as poetry, etc.

10. Many times a writer has understandings about his or her narrative that are implied by the story, but not fully explained. Frequently it is a good idea to share those understandings with the reader and not to take for granted that the reader will be on the same wavelength. The importance of making a traumatized and insecure young girl feel special is emphasized in these paragraphs. These last paragraphs also add the perspective of adult reflection to that of the young girl in the story.

Vocabulary

1. voile (2)—a thin, sheer fabric
2. benign (4)—well-meaning
3. gait (8)—manner of walking
4. morocco-bound (11)—covered in a fine, textured leather
5. chifforobe (17)—a narrow, high chest of drawers
6. infuse (24)—to put in, as by pouring
7. boggled (27)—overwhelmed by complexity
8. leered (32)—a sly, sidelong look displaying ill will
9. homely (35)—simple, crude, ordinary
10. aura (42)—an invisible atmosphere supposedly surrounding a person or thing
11. wormwood (42)—a bitter oil used in making absinthe; therefore, a bitter, unpleasant, or mortifying experience
12. mead (42)—an alcoholic ale

Chapter 13

Writing Essays Using Multiple Strategies

p. 349

■ Summary

Combining Strategies

- strategies are seldom used in isolation
- strategies are various ways to think about a topic
- strategies serve a specific purpose

Choosing the Best Strategies

- questions to help select strategies to match your purpose

Problems to Avoid

- overkill; using all strategies
- illogical organization

Sample Student Essay

Professional Essay

Questions on Content, Structure, and Style, p.358

Suggestions for Writing

Vocabulary

A Revision Worksheet

Reviewing Your Progress

■ Discussion, Answers to Questions, Vocabulary

"Don't Let Stereotypes Warp Your Judgments" by Robert L. Heilbroner—p. 355

Discussion

Students can readily identify with this essay by listing on the board a variety of stereotypes they have experienced either by having judged or by having been judged by others. If they were going to write a similar essay or respond to this one, what specific examples from their experience could they offer? After this discussion, use question 10 below (identifying the different strategies Heilbroner uses) as the basis for a group activity. Divide students into groups and have them list the strategies in the essay and tell why the author has used each at a specific point in the essay. Each group can explain a few paragraphs in a feedback session after this group work.

Answers to Questions, 358

1. Heilbroner uses these questions to call up common stereotypes most readers will share in order to connect readers to the practice of prejudging people. If he were to begin differently, with a definition of prejudice, for example, readers might immediately react that they certainly are not prejudiced. The examples will help readers see they all share some of these sometimes subtle stereotypes.
2. Heilbroner defines a stereotype as "a kind of gossip about the world" that is the basis of prejudice. The studies illustrate that stereotyping is a subconscious, ever-present influence on our perceptions and beliefs.
3. Using first person includes Heilbroner in "those who stereotype" and, by this admission, connects him more closely to the readers who are also a part of "we." By doing so, the essay becomes more of an easily accepted observation on a tendency of human nature rather than a scolding lecture such as "You should not prejudge others."
4. One of the reasons stereotypes develop is that as children we begin "type casting" people, sorting out the "good guys" and the "bad guys." Also, the media perpetuates stereotypes in jokes, characterizations, and advertising. We stereotype to make sense of the confusion of our world, to give definition to the chaos around us.

5. One who stereotypes loses the opportunity to create an individual picture of the world. By seeing the world as so many categories of identical "cutouts" instead of seeing it as diverse and nuanced, the person becomes a stereotype who is totally predictable and inflexible.

6. Heilbroner's opening examples are hypothetical (see answer 1). The specific examples from the studies add concrete support to his claim about the ubiquitous nature of stereotyping. In paragraph 11, the author cites two commonly held stereotypes to explain how we rationalize and confirm our prejudices. Other groups of frequently held stereotypes found in paragraphs 12 and 15 help a reader begin to recognize and question those beliefs.

7. The three-step process in paragraphs 18–20 outlines a way readers can acknowledge complexity and individuality rather than perpetuate stereotypes.

8. These quotations lend authority and a broader perspective than just Heilbroner's to his opinions.

9. The conclusion underscores what the reader has to gain from the essay. The metaphor of paintings in a gallery is a memorable way for the reader to go away with a strong grasp of the overall process of stereotyping; the metaphor condenses the process into a vivid mental picture.

10. Strategies used in the essay:

   Paragraphs 1–3 Hypothetical examples

   Paragraph 4 Specific examples

   Paragraph 5 Definition

   Paragraph 6 Specific examples

   Paragraphs 7–13 Causal analysis

   Paragraphs 15–19 Process analysis

Vocabulary

1. swarthy (4)—dark complexioned
2. dinned (8)—told repeatedly and persistently
3. perpetuated (8)—continued indefinitely
4. synchronized (9)—regulated the timing of
5. semantics (11)—study of the relationship between words and their meanings
6. vindicated (11)—cleared from suspicion or guilt
7. impoverish (12)—to make poor
8. chastening (18)—correcting by punishment
9. edifice (18)—an imposing building
10. chary (19)—shy, cautious

Part 3

Special Assignments

Chapter 14

Writing a Paper Using Research

p. 363

■ Summary

Focusing Your Topic

- some are assigned and already specific and narrowed
- others are more general and need a little or a lot of narrowing

Beginning Your Library Research

- general reference works
- online catalogs
- indexes
- CD-ROMs and databases
- the Internet
- special collections

Conducting Primary Research

- collect first-hand data to obtain information not available from other sources
- interview
- use questionnaires

The Personal Interview

Conducting the Personal Interview

Before the interview

- know your purpose
- make an appointment
- educate yourself about your topic
- plan some questions

During the interview

- make a good first impression
- ask, listen, ask
- be flexible
- ask for more details when necessary and use a friendly tone
- keep to the original topic, when necessary redirect discussion
- conclude thoughtfully and thank the interviewee

After the interview

- review your notes immediately
- consider sending a copy of your work to the interviewee
- send a thank-you note

The Questionnaire

Developing the Questionnaire

- know your purpose and target audience
- encourage participation
- choose the most effective type of questionnaire
  - yes/no answers
  - multiple choice
  - checklist
  - rank order
  - rating system
  - open questions

- watch your language
  - clarify vague references and abbreviations
  - avoid loaded questions
  - focus on one piece of information per question
- keep it short, simple, and smooth

Administering the Questionnaire
- secure a valid sampling
- perform a test run
- prepare ahead—distribution, collection, permissions, materials
- analyze responses
- report findings accurately

Preparing a Working Bibliography
- things to note from sources

Choosing and Evaluating Your Sources

The writer should ask:
- What is the purpose of this Web site?
- What do I know about the publisher, sponsor, creator, author?
- Is my research reasonably balanced? Is the site unbiased?
- Are my sources reporting valid research?
- Are my sources still current?

Preparing an Annotated Bibliography
[Note: Requiring students to compile an annotated bibliography at this stage of the research process may be an effective way of ensuring progress is being made. This might help writers avoid the weak research sources so often found in a frenzied last-minute search.]

Taking Notes
- use index cards—easily organized, research notebook, or computer file
- use photocopies—title pages and bibliographic information with page numbers
- use computer note files—easily transferred into essay draft
- direct quotations
- paraphrase
- summary
- your own ideas

Distinguishing Paraphrase from Summary

- paraphrase: puts information in researcher's own words, follows order of original text, and includes important details
- summary: uses key ideas, omits supporting details, and is much shorter than original

Incorporating Your Source Material

- use your sources in a clear, logical way
- don't overuse direct quotations
- don't "drop in" direct quotations next to your prose
- vary your sentence pattern when you present quotations
- punctuate your quotations correctly
- make certain your support is in your paper
- don't let reference material dominate your essay

Avoiding Plagiarism

Practicing What You've Learned, p. 391

Assignment

Choosing the Documentation Style for Your Essay

MLA Style

- MLA citations in your essay
- compiling a Works Cited list
- sample entries
- electronic sources

APA Style

- APA citations in your essay
- compiling a reference list
- sample entries
- electronic sources

Footnote/Bibliography Form

Using Supplementary Notes

Sample Student Paper Using MLA Style

Student Sample Using APA Style

■ Answers to "Practicing What You've Learned" Exercises

[Users of previous editions should notice that the research in Amy Lawrence's paper has been updated. At the time of publication, bodies were accounted for with the exception of one daughter; there is still controversy over which daughter is missing.]

Practicing What You've Learned, p. 391

1. Bibliography Card

   Ferguson, Wallace K., and Geoffrey Brun. <u>A Survey of European Civilization Part Two, Since 1660</u>. 3rd ed. Boston: Houghton Mifflin Company, 1962. Notes from p. 716.

2. Paraphrase

   Alexander got the title of "Tsar liberator" by freeing 40 million Russian serfs. Rural Russia in the early 1800s was medieval. Less than 100,000 of the nobility held more than nine-tenths of the land. Serfs could be sold, forced to be servants, or sent to factories for the master's own profit. Though some nobles were like kindly fathers to their "children," others overworked their serfs, beat them, and invaded their privacy whenever they wanted. A serf could not get married or leave the estate without permission and would be chased, dragged back, and punished if he did. Basically, a serf was at the mercy of the master.

3. Summary

   Alexander was the tsar who freed 40 million Russian serfs. Russia in the early nineteenth century was medieval in that a minority of noble families held most of the land. Serfs could be sold, told to be servants, or sent to work in factories. Some nobles were good to their serfs, but others abused them. A serf had no rights and could be punished for disobeying the master.

4. In their survey of European civilization, Ferguson and Brun point out that some serfs were "sent to the factories in the towns for their master's profit" (716).

5. Nineteenth-century Russia was still an undemocratic country. Not only was most of the land held by a minority of the nobility, but as Ferguson and Brun note, the peasants (serfs) had no rights and could even "be sold with the estates to new landlords" (716).

Writing in Class: Exams and "Response" Essays

p. 423

■ Summary

Steps to Writing Well Under Pressure

1. Clarify for yourself the kind of task you face.
  - "short answer" exam questions
  - essay exam questions
  - "prompted" essays
  - summary-and-response essays

2. Arrive prepared.
  - bring essential materials such as paper, extra pens and pencils, a stopwatch
  - be courteous to your classmates

3. Read the assignment with great care.

4. Prepare to write.
  - think positively
  - take the first few minutes to think and plan

- after choosing a thesis jot down a brief plan or outline
- budget your time before beginning to write

5. Begin writing, remembering what you have learned about paragraphing, topic sentences, and supporting evidence.
   - write on only one side of the paper
   - try to conclude your essay in a satisfactory way
6. If time allows, read what you have written.
7. Put your name on every page.

Problems to Avoid

- misreading the assignment
- incomplete essay/exam
- composition amnesia
- gorilla generalizations

Practicing What You've Learned, p. 429

Writing the Summary-and-Response Essay

Reading the Assignment and the Article

- determine what you are being asked to do
- thoroughly understand the ideas in the assigned reading
- study and annotate articles if given the opportunity ahead of time

Writing the Summary Section

- treat the article's ideas objectively
- include the author's name and the title of the article
- paraphrase

Writing the Response Section

- check your notes
- determine your overall assessment
- plan your organization
- transition smoothly between sections
- use tag lines
- use supporting evidence
- include a critique of author's logic, style, or tone if allowed
- conclude consistently with your overall assessment

Sample Student Essay

Practicing What You've Learned, p. 435

Assignment

■ Answers to "Practicing What You've Learned" Exercises

Practicing What You've Learned, p. 429

1. Underline "flower imagery" and "major theme . . . <u>The Bluest Eye.</u>" Circle "Discuss," "examples," and "clarify." Example, causal analysis, or argument.
2. Underline "the Bay of Pigs . . . Cuba." Circle "Trace" and "the events that led to." Causal analysis, description.
3. Underline "Louis B. Mayer" and "American Film . . . of Moviemaking." Circle "Discuss" and "major influences on." Causal analysis, description, argument.
4. Underline "The 1957 . . . system." Circle "Agree or disagree." Argument.
5. Underline "the surrealistic . . . Dali" and "important . . . artists." Circle "Consider the similarities . . . between" and "Illustrate . . . references to." Compare/contrast, example.

Practicing What You've Learned, p. 435
Student responses will vary.

Chapter **16**

Writing about Literature

p. 437

■ Summary

Using Literature in the Classroom

- prompts: using literature as a springboard for an essay
- literary analysis: interpretation of a piece of literature

Suggestions for Close Reading of Literature

- read and reread
- annotate
- dispel myth about "hidden meanings"
- seek ways to reasonably support your own interpretation

Steps to Reading a Story

- check biographical information
- read story once for plot
- look up important vocabulary words
- make preliminary notes on major themes
- analyze story's parts and reason for each; evaluate point of view

- analyze structure of story
- analyze characters
- examine setting and its import
- study language use: figurative language, symbols, style, and tone
- review and refine initial reactions

Annotated Story

Sample Student Essay

Steps to Reading a Poem

- check biographical information
- read poem at least twice; paraphrase poem; analyze sentences and vocabulary
- decide if poem is narrative or lyrical; determine dominant idea
- analyze narrator of poem
- examine the setting or occasion of poem
- analyze characters
- examine the poem's word choice
- analyze the structure of the poem
- examine the sound devices
- analyze the rhythm
- review and refine initial reactions

Annotated Poem

Sample Student Essay

Guidelines for Writing about Literature

- select a workable topic
- present a clear thesis
- follow literary conventions
- organize effectively
- use ample evidence
- find a pleasing conclusion

Problems to Avoid

- don't assign meanings; show evidence of your interpretation
- don't drop in quoted lines without explaining them
- don't rehash the plot in summary; don't neglect analysis

Practicing What You've Learned, pp. 455, 462

■ Answers to "Practicing What You've Learned" Exercises

Practicing What You've Learned, p. 455

"Geraldo No Last Name" by Sandra Cisneros

In "Geraldo No Last Name," Cisneros uses terse, or clipped, sentence structures to focus the reader on the brevity of the relationship between the girl and the boy who is killed by a hit and run driver. The girl's lack of knowledge about the boy has her filling in bits of information that she assumes from looking at him. The stereotyping stems from her lack of knowledge and it may in fact contribute to why she never got to know this boy with whom she danced regularly. But the quality of not seeing beyond our own needs and desires can also lead to maintaining a distance and relying on stereotypes as a way to relate to others. In this sense, Geraldo could be anyone.

"The Cask of Amontillado" by Edgar Allan Poe

In "The Cask of Amontillado," Poe's narrator is speaking to someone who "knows his soul so well," and thus, since he is also telling the tale from the perspective of events that happened in the past, we might assume he is confessing to his priest, perhaps on his own deathbed, as it is a "half-century" that has passed that "no moral" has disturbed the pile of bones he replaced in front of Fortunato's grave. In other words, he has had no remorse until his present telling, and even then, his sincerity is suspect. He could be simply fantasizing about revenge, or about confessing. If he is fantasizing about revenge, then the piece becomes an elaborate psychodrama. If he is fantasizing about confessing, the psychodrama takes on added comprehension about his character. We could then view Montresor as assassinating his own character, as well or in place of Fortunato. Evidence of his similarity in character to Fortunato's is addressed early on when he compares their communal penchant for good wine. And, since a cask of wine is what takes them both to the tombs, there may be an attempt to singularly address his loss of "fortune" to the purchase of drink, so that his confession becomes a metaphor and an explanation to heirs. There are a number of ways to read this short story, but if we consider the narrator reliable, we can assume the first impression noted above. If we consider that drink has addled his brain, we might assume the story is a fantasy and Montresor an unreliable narrator. The criteria for his actions are an insult, which is not named, and a family motto that commands him to avenge such insult. There are a number of ironic statements, but the main is in Fortunato compelling Montresor to take him to the cellar, thus guaranteeing his own demise.

Practicing What You've Learned, p. 462

"Those Winter Sundays" by Robert Hayden and "The Road Not Taken" by Robert Frost

The point of view in both of these poems is first person and the speakers are adults, perhaps middle aged for both have an ability to reflect on the past. Frost's speaker assumes he will look back on his action in later years, while Hayden's speaker seems new to understanding the father's behavior when the speaker was a child. This understanding also seems to have come after the father has died or because the speaker has become a parent. Hayden describes the father's work and attention to his family's needs. Frost describes choosing a path in life, one that was hard but not unsatisfying. Hayden's language is cold and hard where there is misunderstanding in the speaker's perspective—"*blueblack cold,*" "*cra*cked hands," "*c*old splin*t*ering," "brea*k*ing," and "*ch*ronic anger." The imagery smoothens with sound as well in "*love's austere* and *lonely offices*" in the speaker's retrospective comprehension of parental love and duty.

Frost's roads as a metaphor for life's choices suggests that the path that most choose is safe but perhaps not as adventurous. Neither are "trodden black" nor unworthy choices, but once either is followed, returning to the same moment/place of choice will not likely happen.

Suggestions for Writing

Some Last Thoughts about Literature

Writing about Visual Arts
p. 467

■ Summary

- artistic visual images enrich our lives
- we learn to analyze through writing
- we need to scrutinize visual images

Using Visual Arts in the Composition Classroom

- personal response
- formal analysis
- strategy practice
- prompted response

Suggestions for Analyzing Paintings

- prepare for your viewing
- note first impressions
- record basic information

- study the subject matter
  - scenes with one or more figures
  - a portrait
  - a landscape
  - a still life
- nonrepresentational art
  - beyond realism
- analyze composition and design
  - arrangement of subject matter/focal point
  - balance of subject matter
  - symbolism
  - light and shadow
  - colors and effects
  - lines and shape—regularity
  - medium used
  - brush strokes
  - pigmentation
  - texture
  - identify period style or "school"

Additional Advice about Sculpture and Photography

Sculptures

- form—time and place
- subject type
- cultural expression
- pose
- materials
- angles of view
- placement, positioning, environment

Photography

- purpose
- name of photographer, photo, subject matter, place and date of photo, place of publication or exhibition

- composition and circumstances or methods used to affect a response
  - lighting
  - color or the absence of
  - exposure time
  - depth of field
  - angle and range of vision
  - focus
  - arrangement of subject matter

Practicing What You've Learned, p. 479

Guidelines for Writing about Art Works

- use a catchy lead-in
- write a compelling thesis
- present an overview of the work
- organize main points effectively
- provide clear supporting evidence
- conclude gracefully

Problems to Avoid

- pay close attention to the assignment
- use vivid description to inform and delight

Annotated Painting: *Nighthawks*

Sample Student Essay

Suggestions for Writing

■ Answers to "Practicing What You've Learned" Exercises

Practicing What You've Learned, p. 479

Answers will vary.

Chapter 18

Writing about Film

p. 487

■ Summary

Using Film in the Composition Classroom

- prompted response
- review essay
- strategy practice
- formal analysis

Guidelines for Writing about Film

- pay close attention to your assignment
- prepare in advance of your first screening
- arrange multiple viewing opportunities
- take notes both as you watch and immediately after, while your memory is fresh
- review your notes in light of your assignment's purpose
- watch the film again with an analytical eye
- consider conventions used in writing about film
- use clear, precise language
- proofread for accuracy in details and mechanics, including citing sources

Problems to Avoid

- don't "pun and run"; explain your views
- don't allow a plot summary to dominate your discussion; have a purpose in mind

Sample Student Essay

Practicing What You've Learned, p. 496

"Cat in the Hat Coughs Up Mayhem" by David Germain

Although this film review includes a thesis and enough witticisms to keep readers entertained, it does not offer enough supporting evidence for the opinions that are given. So students can learn to add supporting details, have them offer specific examples for Germain's ideas. For instance, what statements or activities cause Myers's performance to be "distasteful" and "hard to endure" (3)? Why are the characters "unpleasant"? Help students to differentiate between the type of opinion that attacks or praises and the type that entails supporting evidence for one's views.

Suggestions for Writing

Glossary of Film Terms

Chapter 19

Writing in the World of Work

p. 501

■ Summary

Composing Business Letters

- determine the main purpose of this letter
- determine the audience. What should he/she know, understand, or decide to do after reading this letter?
- decide what impression of yourself you want to present

Business Letter Format

- heading
- inside address
- salutation
- text

- complimentary closing
- signature
- notes such as encl., cc, xc, c when appropriate
- avoid postscripts
- proofread

Practicing What You've Learned, page 506

Assignment

Sample Business Letter

Creating Memos

- a common form of brief communication within a business or organization
- clear and concise

Sending Professional E-mail

- use a helpful subject line
- begin with an appropriate greeting
- be brief
- ease eyestrain; keep paragraphs short and skip lines between
- use a polite, friendly tone and clear, precise words
- use a closing appropriate to the audience
- revise, proofread, copy, send

Problems to Avoid

- remember that business e-mail is not private
- don't shout by using all caps
- don't use abbreviations or emoticons
- don't forward other people's e-mail without permission
- think twice before you write

Designing Résumés

- functional format places the reader's focus on the applicant's education and skills
- experiential format emphasizes work history
- include heading
- include employment objective
- include education history: schools, locations, majors, minors, date of degrees

- list professional experience
- note skills
- include honors, awards, activities
- provide references, persons to contact for more information
- add personal information thoughtfully

Critique Your Page Appeal

- use high-quality paper
- balance text and white space
- arrange material in an engaging way
- proofread

Problems to Avoid

- never lie
- contact your references in advance and thank them after in a note
- add personal information thoughtfully
- consider providing keywords (and simple formats, clear fonts) for scanning software

Assignment

Sample Résumés

Preparing Interview Notes and Post-Interview Letters

■ Answers to "Practicing What You've Learned" Exercises

Practicing What You've Learned, p. 506

Answers will vary.

Part 4

A Concise Handbook

Chapter 20

Major Errors in Grammar

p. 521

■ Summary

Errors with Verbs

- faulty agreement
- subjunctive
- tense shift
- split infinitive
- double negatives
- passive voice

Errors with Nouns

- possessive with "-ing" nouns
- misuse of nouns as adjectives
- plurals of proper nouns

Errors with Pronouns

- faulty agreement
- vague reference
- shift in pronouns
- incorrect case
- incorrect compound forms

Practicing What You've Learned, p. 531

Errors with Adverbs and Adjectives

- incorrect usage
- faulty comparison

Practicing What You've Learned, p. 534

Errors in Modifying Phrases

- dangling modifiers
- misplaced modifiers

Practicing What You've Learned, p. 535

Errors in Sentences

- fragments

Practicing What You've Learned, p. 537

- run-on sentence

Practicing What You've Learned, p. 539

- comma splice

Practicing What You've Learned, p. 540

- faulty parallelism

Practicing What You've Learned, p. 542

- false predication
- mixed structure

Practicing What You've Learned, p. 544

■ Answers to "Practicing What You've Learned" Exercises

Errors with Verbs

Practicing What You've Learned, p. 523

A. 1. A recent report on Cuban land crabs <u>shows</u> they can run faster than horses.
2. The team from Snooker Hollow High School <u>is</u> considering switching from basketball to basket weaving because passing athletics is now required for graduation.
3. Neither of the students <u>knows</u> that both mystery writer Agatha Christie and inventor Thomas Edison <u>were</u> dyslexic.
4. Each of the twins <u>has</u> read about Joseph Priestley's contribution to the understanding of oxygen, but neither <u>was</u> aware that he also invented the pencil eraser.
5. Clarity in speech and writing <u>is</u> absolutely essential in the business world today.
6. Some scholars believe that the world's first money, in the form of coins, <u>was</u> made in Libya, a country that is now part of Turkey.
7. Bananas, rich in vitamins and low in fats, <u>are</u> rated the most popular fruit in America.
8. There <u>are</u> many children in this country who appreciate a big plate of hot grits, but none of the Hall children <u>likes</u> this Southern dish.
9. Either the cocker spaniel or the poodle <u>holds</u> the honor of being the most popular breed of dogs in the United States, <u>says</u> the American Kennel Club.
10. Many people <u>consider</u> Johnny Appleseed a mythical figure, but now two local historians, authors of a well-known book on the subject, <u>argue</u> that he was a real person named John Chapman.

Practicing What You've Learned, p. 526

A. 1. He could hardly wait to hear country music star Sue Flay sing her version of his favorite song, "I've Been Flushed from the Bathroom of Your Heart."
2. "If you were in Wyoming and couldn't hear the wind blowing, what would people call you?" asked Jethro. "Dead," replied his buddy Herman.
3. The Aztec ruler Montezuma believed that chocolate had magical powers and could act as an aphrodisiac.
4. Tammy's favorite band is Opie Gone Bad, so she always buys their concert tickets, even though she can't afford to.
5. The Fire Department is raising suspicions of arson following the burning of the new Chip and Dale Furniture Factory. (Or, "Following the burning of the new Chip and Dale Furniture Factory, the Fire Department is raising suspicions of arson.")

Practicing What You've Learned, p. 526

B. 1. I saw what she was hiding behind her back.
    2. He came around here yesterday asking questions, but we're used to that.
    3. Having forgotten the combination to the safe, the burglar quietly sneaked out the back door. (Snuck is dialectical.)
    4. Austin doesn't like to be awakened until noon.
    5. The kids did good work all day.

Errors with Nouns and Pronouns

Practicing What You've Learned, p. 531

A. 1. Please buy a copy of the book *The Celery Stalks at Midnight* for my sister and <u>me</u>.
    2. Between you and <u>me</u>, some people define a Freudian slip as saying one thing but meaning your mother.
    3. <u>Who</u> is the singer of the country song "You Can't Make a Heel Toe the Mark"?
    4. Aunt Beulah makes better cookies than <u>I</u>.
    5. <u>He and I</u> are going to the movies to see *Attack of the Killer Crabgrass*.
    6. I'm giving my accordion to <u>whomever</u> is carrying a grudge against our neighbors.
    7. The Botox surprise party was given by Paige Turner, Justin Case, and <u>me</u>.
    8. She is the kind of person for <u>whom</u> housework meant sweeping the room with a glance.
    9. <u>She and he</u> are twins.
   10. The judge of the ugly feet contest found choosing between <u>him and her</u> too difficult.

B. 1. Clarence and <u>I</u> have an uncle who is so mean that he writes the name of the murderer on the first page of mystery novels that are passed around the family.
    2. Correct.
    3. It was a surprise to both Mary and <u>me</u> to learn that Switzerland didn't give women the right to vote until 1971.
    4. Each of the young women in the Family Life class decided not to marry after <u>she</u> read that couples today have 2.3 children.
    5. Correct.
    6. Those of us who'd had the flu agreed that <u>one</u> can always get a doctor to return <u>one's</u> call more quickly if <u>one</u> gets in the shower; but let's keep this tip confidential between you and <u>me</u>.
    7. The stranger gave the free movie tickets to Louise and <u>me</u> after he saw people standing in line to leave the theater.
    8. The personnel director told <u>each</u> of the employees, most of whom opposed him, to signify <u>his</u> or <u>her</u> "no" vote by saying, "I resign."
    9. <u>People</u> know <u>they're</u> in trouble when <u>their</u> salary undergoes a modification reduction adjustment of 50 percent.
   10. One of the first movies to gross over one million dollars was *Tarzan of the Apes* (1932), starring Johnny Weismuller, a former Olympic star who became an actor. <u>Such a large profit</u> didn't happen often in the movie industry at that time. (Or, At that time, it was unusual for Olympic champions to become movie stars.)

Errors with Adverbs and Adjectives

Practicing What You've Learned, p. 534

A. 1. After the optometrist pulled her eye tooth, Hortense didn't behave very <u>well</u> in the waiting room.
  2. Which is the <u>worst</u> food—liver or buttermilk?
  3. I didn't do <u>well</u> on my nature project because my bonsai sequoia tree grew <u>badly</u> in its tiny container.
  4. Don't forget to dress <u>warmly</u> for the Arctic Freestyle Race.
  5. Of the twins, Teensie is more <u>fun</u> than Egore.
  6. Watching Joe Bob eat candied fruit flies made Jolene feel <u>really</u> ill, and his table manners did not make her feel <u>better</u>.
  7. The Roman toothpick holder was <u>unique</u>.
  8. That was the <u>funniest</u> flea circus I have ever seen.
  9. Does the instructional guide *Bobbing for Doughnuts* still sell <u>well</u>?
  10. The Fighting Mosquitoes were trained <u>well</u>, but they just didn't take practices <u>seriously</u>.

Errors in Modifying Phrases

Practicing What You've Learned, p. 535

A. 1. After tasting the meals on Hard Luck Airlines, we decided to return home via ship.
  2. To report a fire, please use the fire department's new phone number found on the enclosed sticker, which can be displayed prominently on your telephone.
  3. The prize-winning sculptor celebrated her $10,000 purchase of a new open-air studio in Aspen, where she lives with her infant daughter.
  4. Showing off letters strewn over his desk, the movie star noted they were all from admirers.
  5. Running too fast during a game of "Kick the Can," I collided with the flagpole.
  6. Eloise bought a computer with a faulty memory from her neighbor.
  7. From her closet, Jean tossed the baggy, wrinkled, and hopelessly out-of-style skirt.
  8. Forgetting to pack underwear, Jonas had to reopen his already bulging suitcase.
  9. Next spring at Slippery Rock College, Blanche will teach a course that incorporates her research into the mating habits of Big Foot.
  10. Discovering that Kate had spent all night in the library, her friends knew she would need a trip to Special Coffee.
  11. Squeezing the can, Dee Dee thought the tomatoes weren't quite ripe.
  12. For the first year of their lives, children don't require solid food.
  13. He doubted the old bicycles would make it over the mountains.
  14. In a book from the public library, I read that a number of modern sailors, like Thor Heyerdahl, have sailed primitive vessels across the ocean.
  15. By proofreading carefully, you can easily spot and correct dangling modifiers.

Fragment Sentence Errors

Practicing What You've Learned, p. 537

A. "It is true that" the following are fragments.

1. Which was in the middle of the Great Depression when money was scarce.
2. As recorded by the United Drive-in Theater Owners Association.
3. Perhaps because escalating land prices make property too valuable for use in this way. Or the fact that they are only open during the summer months.
4. Including the American territories, too.
5. For instance, the miniature golf industry, down from 50,000 courses in the 1930s to fewer than 15,000 today.

B. 1. According to Lawrence M. Ausbel, author of "Credit Cards" in *The McGrawHill Encyclopedia of Economics,* the idea of a credit card first appeared in 1887.
2. Originally an imaginary concept in a futurist novel by Edward Bellamy, the card allowed characters to charge against future earnings.
3. Around the turn of the century, some American stores issued paper or metal "shop-pers' plates," although they were used only by retailers to identify their credit cus-tomers.
4. The first real credit card was issued in 1947 by a New York bank and was a success, despite the fact that customers could charge only purchases in a two-block area in Brooklyn.
5. Travel and entertainment cards soon appeared, including the American Express card in 1958 and Carte Blanche in 1959, which allowed customers to charge items and ser-vices across the country.

Run-on Sentence

Practicing What You've Learned, p. 539

Run-ons

1. While workers in the United States take an average of thirteen days of vacation a year, in Italy they take forty-two.
2. In 1901, a school teacher named Annie Edson Taylor became the first person to go over Niagara Falls in a wooden barrel; she is the only woman known to survive this risky adventure.
3. Before the choir sang "Break Forth into Joy," the minister preached his farewell sermon.
4. The first microwave oven marketed in 1959 was a built-in unit that cost a whopping $2,595.
5. Coffee was considered a food in the Middle Ages, and travelers who found it growing in Ethiopia mixed with animal fat.

Comma Splice Errors

Practicing What You've Learned, p. 540

A. 1. Most people know that the likeness of Susan B. Anthony appeared on an American dollar coin in the 1990s, but fewer people know exactly who she was or why she is so important.

   2. For most of her life Anthony fought for a woman's right to achieve the vote; she was an organizer of the world's first women's rights convention in 1848.

   3. Anthony often risked her safety and her freedom for her beliefs, sometimes being arrested, as she was in 1872 for the crime of voting in an election.

   4. She also worked to secure laws to protect working women, whose wages, at that time, automatically belonged to their husbands.

   5. Unfortunately, Anthony did not live to see the 1920 passage of the Nineteenth Amendment, that gave women the right to vote—she died in 1906.

B. 1. My mother is very politically conservative; she's written in George III for president in the last two elections.

   2. Mary Lou decided not to eat the alphabet soup because the letters spelled out "botulism."

   3. A dried gourd containing seeds probably functioned as the first baby rattle. Ancient Egyptian wall paintings show babies with such gourds clutched in their fingers.

   4. Opportunists who came to the South after the Civil War were often called "carpet-baggers" since they carried their belongings in cheaply produced travel bags made of Belgian carpet.

   5. A friend of mine offers a good definition of nasty theater critics on opening night. According to him, they're the people who can't wait to stone the first cast.

   6. The Smithsonian Institution was started when English scientist James Smithson died in 1829 and willed his entire fortune to the United States to establish a foundation for knowledge.

   7. The word "jack-o'-lantern" may have come from the legend of Irish Jack. A mean old man in life, he was condemned after death to wander the earth carrying a hollow turnip with a lump of burning coal inside.

   8. Americans forget how large the blue whale is. It has a heart as large as a Volkswagen Beetle and can hold an elephant on its tongue.

   9. Correct.

   10. The famous Eiffel Tower, built for the 1889 Paris Exposition, has inspired many crazy stunts: in 1891, Silvain Domon climbed the 363 steps on stilts.

Errors in Parallelism

Practicing What You've Learned, p. 542

   1. Is it true that Superman could leap tall buildings, run faster than a locomotive, and deflect bullets with his skin?

   2. To celebrate the canned meat product called Spam, we attended the Texas Spamarama Festival to participate in the Spambalaya cook-off, the Spam-can toss, and the Spam-jam Jazz session. Later, we danced to such favorites as "Twist and Snout."

3. My Aunt Clara swears she has seen Elvis snacking at the deli, browsing at the super-market, munching at the pizza parlor, and reading in the cookbook section of the local bookstore.
4. According to my husband, summer air in Louisiana is one percent oxygen, nine percent water, and ninety percent mosquitoes.
5. Many teachers believe that the most important keys to success for students in college include attending class, keeping up with reading, and being brave enough to ask questions. (Option: . . . *attending class, reading assigned material, and asking questions.*)
6. Yoga encourages its participants to work on increasing flexibility and strength while decreasing stress.
7. Drivers should eliminate distractions such as eating, drinking, using the cell phone, and changing radio stations.
8. Smart people learn from their own mistakes; smarter people learn from others' mistakes.
9. Theater class helped me to overcome shyness, to make new friends, and to engage in other activities.
10. The writer Oscar Wilde, the dancer Isadora Duncan, the painter Max Ernst, and the rock star Jim Morrison are all buried in the same Paris cemetery.

Errors of False Predication and Mixed Structure

Practicing What You've Learned, p. 544

1. The team quarterback, A. M. Hall, who broke his finger and was sidelined last week for the Raiders' game, is expected to play in tonight's game.
2. The groom, a graduate of Centerville High School, has lived in Centerville all of his life.
3. On my way to the doctor's office, my car's universal joint went out, which caused me even more body damage, when I steered into a tree.
4. When he brought home a twenty-pound block of ice after ice fishing all day, he revealed his intelligence.
5. The town offers low-cost daycare services to new residents with children.
6. Nineteenth century cynic Ambrose Bierce noted that marriage entails "a master, a mis-tress, and two slaves, making in all, two."
7. When the plumber shows up three hours late, I get mad.
8. I owe some of my success as an actor to my drama teacher.
9. Because sound travels slower than light, the advice parents give their teenagers should reach them about the time they turn forty.
10. He was found in a ditch near some stray cows when a passerby heard his cries for help. (*Or: Some strays cows heard his cries for help and found him in a ditch.*)

Chapter 21

A Concise Guide to Punctuation
p. 545

■ Summary

The Colon

Practicing What You've Learned, p. 555

The Apostrophe

Practicing What You've Learned, p. 557

Quotation Marks

Practicing What You've Learned, p. 560

Parentheses

Brackets

The Dash

Practicing What You've Learned, p. 563

The Hyphen

Practicing What You've Learned, p. 565

Italics and Underlining

Practicing What You've Learned, p. 566

Ellipsis Points

The Slash

Practicing What You've Learned, p. 568

■ Answers to "Practicing What You've Learned" Exercises

Errors Using Periods, Question Marks, and Exclamation Points

Practicing What You've Learned, p. 546

1. The space program sent some cows into orbit last year. I think they are now known as the herd shot around the world.
2. Ms. Anita Bath wants to know why erasers never outlast their pencils.
3. Her French class at St. Clair's School on First Ave. was taught by Madame Beau V. Rhee, Ph.D.

4. Where do all the birds go when it's raining?
5. I have wonderful news. I won the lottery!

Comma Errors

Practicing What You've Learned, p. 551

A. 1. In 1886, temperance leader Harvey Wilcox left Kansas and purchased 120 acres near Los Angeles to develop a new town.
   2. Although there were no holly trees growing in that part of California, Mrs. Wilcox named the area Hollywood.
   3. Mrs. Wilcox may have named the place after a friend's summer home that was located in Illinois.
   4. During the early years, settlers who shared the Wilcoxes' values moved to the area and banned the recreational drinking of alcoholic beverages. However, some alcohol consumption was allowed for medicinal purposes.
   5. Nevertheless, by 1910 the first film studio opened its doors inside a tavern on Sunset Boulevard. Within seven short years, the quiet community started by the Wilcoxes had vanished.

B. 1. Yes, Hortense, in the 1920s young women did indeed cut their hair, raise their hemlines, dab perfume behind their knees, and dance the Charleston.
   2. In 1873, Cornell University canceled the school's first intercollegiate football game with Michigan when the president announced, "I will not permit 30 men to travel 400 miles merely to agitate a bag of wind."
   3. Jane, Marian, Donna, Ann, and Cissy graduated from high school on June 5, 1964, in Texarkana, Texas, in the old Walnut Street Auditorium.
   4. "I may be a man of few opinions," said Henry, "but I insist that I am neither for nor against apathy."
   5. Did you know, for instance, that early American settlers once thought the tomato was so poisonous they only used the plant for decoration?

C. 1. The father decided to recapture his youth, so he took his son's car keys away.
   2. Although ice cream didn't appear in America until the 1700s, our country now leads the world in ice cream consumption, but Australia is second, I think.
   3. Last summer, the large, friendly family that lives next door flew Discount Airlines and visited three cities on their vacation; however, their suitcases visited five.
   4. Researchers in Balboa, Panama, have discovered that the poisonous, yellow-belly sea snake, which descended from the cobra, is the most deadly serpent in the world.
   5. Lulu Belle, my cousin, spent the week of September 1–7, 1986, in the woods near Dimebox, Texas, looking for additions to her extinct butterfly collection. However, she wasn't at all successful in her search.

Semicolon Errors

Practicing What You've Learned, p. 553

1. The soloist sang the well-known hymn "I Will Not Pass This Way Again" at her concert last night; the audience was delighted.
2. Apples have long been associated with romance. For example, one legend says if you throw an apple peel over your shoulder, it will fall into the shape of your true love's initial.

3. According to an 1863 book of etiquette, the perfect hostess will see to it that the works of male and female authors are properly separated on her bookshelves; however, if the authors happen to be married, their proximity may be tolerated.
4. Today, there are some 60,000 Americans older than 100; in 1960, there were only 3,222, according to <u>Health</u> magazine.
5. The sixth-grade drama club will present its interpretation of <u>Hamlet</u> tonight in the school cafeteria; all parents are invited to see this tragedy.
6. Some inventors who named weapons after themselves include Samuel Colt, the Colt revolver; Henry Deringer Jr., the derringer pistol; Dr. Richard Gatling, the crank machine gun: Col. John T. Thompson, the submachine or "tommy" gun; and Oliver F. Winchester, the repeating rifle.
7. My doctor failed in his career as a kidnapper; no one could read his ransom notes.
8. The highest point in the United States is Mt. McKinley at 20,320 feet; in contrast, the lowest point is Death Valley at 282 feet below sea level.
9. As we drove down the highway, we saw a sign that said "See the World's Largest Prairie Dog. Turn Right at This Exit"; therefore, we immediately stopped to look.
10. The next billboard read "See Live Jackalopes," making us want to stop again.

Errors with Colons

Practicing What You've Learned, p. 555

1. Experts have discovered over 30 different kinds of clouds but have separated them into three main types: cirrus, cumulus, and stratus.
2. Correct.
3. A recent Gallup poll found that Americans only consider one activity more stressful than visiting the dentist: hosting a dinner party.
4. Because Hindu custom forbids the eating of beef, McDonald's restaurants in India often feature veggie burgers and mutton burgers.
5. Please remember to buy the following at the pet store: one pound of cat food, two flea collars, kitty fang floss, a bag of catnip, and thirty-six lint rollers.
6. The Director of Academic Services at Pennsylvania State University once nominated this sentence for Outstanding Grammar Error of the Year: "I had to leave my good friend's behind and find new ones."
7. Some of the cars manufactured between 1907 and 1912 that didn't achieve the popularity of the Model T were the Black Crow, the Swallow, the Bugmobile, and the Carnation.
8. There's only one thing that can make our lawn look as good as our neighbor's: snow.
9. In a Thurmont, Maryland cemetery can be found this epitaph: "Here lies an Atheist, all dressed up and no place to go."
10. George Bernard Shaw, the famous playwright, claimed he wanted the following epitaph on his tombstone: "I knew if I stayed around long enough, something like this would happen."

Errors with Apostrophes

Practicing What You've Learned, p. 557

A. 1. A horse's pajamas
   2. The queen's throne
   3. A family's vacation

   4. Ten students' grades
   5. The Depression of the 1930's [or 1930s] was over.
   6. That dress of hers
   7. The children's toys
   8. Worms for sale
   9. Bill Jones' (or Jones's) car
   10. All essays are due today.
   11. Sign both the roofer's and the painter's contracts.
   12. Women's hats with feathers for decoration
B. 1. It's unfortunate that the game ended in a tie.
   2. The tree lost its leaves.
   3. It's beginning to feel like fall now.
   4. The library was closing its doors.
   5. I realize it's none of my business.

Errors with Apostrophes and Quotation Marks

Practicing What You've Learned, p. 560

   1. It's true that when famous wit Dorothy Parker was told that President Coolidge, also known as "Silent Cal," was dead, she exclaimed, "How can they tell?"
   2. When a woman seated next to Coolidge at a dinner party once told him she had made a bet with a friend that she could get more than two words out of him, he replied, "You lose."
   3. Twenty-one of Elvis Presley's albums have sold over a million copies; twenty of The Beatles' albums have also done so.
   4. Cinderella's stepmother wasn't pleased that her daughter received an "F" in her creative writing class on her poem "Seven Guys and a Gal," which she had plagiarized from her two friends Snow White and Dopey.
   5. "Wasn't it Mae West who said, 'When choosing between two evils, I always like to try the one I've never tried before'?" asked Olivia.
   6. Horace said, "Believe me, it's to everybody's advantage to sing the popular song 'You Stole My Heart and Stomped That Sucker Flat,' if that's what the holdup man wants."
   7. A scholar's research has revealed that the five most commonly used words in written English are "the," "of," "and," "a," and "to." (Underlining the words in quotation marks would also be correct.)
   8. The triplets' mother said that while it's hard for her to choose, O. Henry's famous short story "The Ransom of Red Chief" is probably her favorite.
   9. Despite both her lawyers' advice, she used the words "terrifying," "hideous," and "unforget-table" to describe her latest flight on Golden Fleece Airways, piloted by Jack "One-Eye" Marcus. (Underlining "terrifying," "hideous," and "unforgettable" would also be correct.)
   10. It's clear that Bubba didn't know if the Christmas tree thrown in the neighbors' yard was ours, theirs, or yours.

Errors with Parentheses, Brackets, and Dashes

Practicing What You've Learned, p. 563

   1. Correct.
   2. . . . [Editor's note: For help with apostrophes, see pages 509–510 in this text.]

3. . . . (sixteen pairs of twins, seven sets of triplets, and four sets of quadruplets).
4. . . . childrens [sic] . . . .
5. . . . his cards right—his Visa card, his Mastercard, his American Express card.

Errors with Hyphens

Practicing What You've Learned, p. 565

1. first-class event
2. well-done steak
3. self-employed person
4. Correct
5. one-word answer
6. Correct
7. once-in-a-lifetime experience
8. fifteen-year-old girl
9. overly excited
10. fifty-sixth birthday
11. Correct
12. The hard-boiled detective omitted an important detail in his report.

Errors with Italics and Underlining

Practicing What You've Learned, p. 566

1. page six of the *New York Times*
2. the popular novel *The Great Gatsby*
3. an article in *Time* magazine
4. watching the episode "The Puffy Shirt" on *Seinfeld*
5. movie stars in *The Matrix*
6. Correct
7. the first act of *Death of a Salesman*
8. remembering the words to "The Star-Spangled Banner"
9. the sinking of the *Edmund Fitzgerald*
10. Correct

Errors with Parentheses, Brackets, Dashes, Hyphens, Underlining, and Ellipses

Practicing What You've Learned, p. 568

1. Many moviegoers know that the ape in *King Kong* (the original 1933 version, not the remake) was only an eighteen-inch-tall animated figure, but not everyone realizes that the Red Sea Moses parted in the 1923 movie of *The Ten Commandments* was a quivering slab of Jell-O sliced down the middle.
2. We recall the last words of General John B. Sedwick at the Battle of Spotsylvania in 1864: "They couldn't hit an elephant at this dist . . ."
3. In a person-to-person telephone call, the twenty-five-year-old starlet promised the hard-working gossip columnist that she would "tell the truth and nothing but the truth" about her highly publicized feud with her ex-husband, editor-in-chief of *Meat-Eaters' Digest.*

4. While sailing across the Atlantic aboard the celebrity-filled yacht the *Titanic II,* Dottie Mae Haskell (she's the author of the popular new self-help book *Finding Wolves to Raise Your Children*) confided that until recently, she thought "chutzpa" was an Italian side dish. (Dashes instead of parentheses would be correct too.)

5. During their twenty-four-hour sit-in at the melt-down site, the anti-nuclear protesters began to sing, "Oh, say can you see . . ."

6. Few people know that James Arness (later Matt Dillon in the long-running television series *Gunsmoke*) got his start by playing the vegetable creature in the postwar monster movie *The Thing* (1951). (For more emphasis, substitute dashes for the parentheses.)

7. If you do not pay your rent on time, your landlord has the right to charge a late fee and/or begin an eviction procedure.

8. A French chemist named Georges Claude invented the first neon sign in 1910. (For additional information on his successful attempts to use seawater to generate electricity, see pp. 200–205.)

9. When Lucille Ball, star of *I Love Lucy,* became pregnant with her first child, the network executives decided that the word *expecting* could be used on the air to refer to her condition, but not the word *pregnant.* ("Expecting" and "pregnant" are also correct.)

10. In mystery stories, the detective often advises the police to *cherchez la femme.* [Editor's note: *Cherchez la femme* means "look for the woman" in French.]

Chapter 22

A Concise Guide to Mechanics

p. 569

■ Summary

Capitalization

Practicing What You've Learned, p. 571

Abbreviations

Numbers

Practicing What You've Learned, p. 574

Spelling

■ Answers to "Practicing What You've Learned" Exercises

Errors with Capitalization

Practicing What You've Learned, p. 571

A. 1. delicious Chinese food
   2. Memorial Day memories
   3. fiery Southwestern salsa
   4. his latest novel, *The Story of a Prince among Thieves*
   5. Bible study at the Baptist church
   6. Count Dracula's castle in Transylvania
   7. African-American heritage
   8. a Dodge van driven across the Golden Gate Bridge
   9. Sunday morning newspapers
   10. the British daughter-in-law of Senator Snort

B. Answers will vary.

Errors in Capitalization, Abbreviations, and Numbers

Practicing What You've Learned, p. 574

1. Speaking to students at Gallaudet University, Marian Wright Edelman, founder and president of the Children's Defense Fund, noted that an American child is born into poverty every 30 seconds, is born to a teen mother every 60 seconds, is abused or neglected every 26 seconds, is arrested for a violent crime every 5 minutes, and is killed by a gun every 2 hours.
2. My sister, who lives in the East, was amazed to read studies by Thomas Radecki, M.D., showing that twelve-year-olds commit 300% more murders than did the same age group thirty years ago.
3. In 67 C.E. the Roman Emperor Nero entered the chariot race at the Olympic Games, and although he failed to finish the race, the judges unanimously declared him the winner.
4. According to John Alcock, a behavioral ecologist at Arizona State University, in the U.S.A. the chances of being poisoned by a snake are twenty times less than those of being hit by lightning and three hundred times less than the risk of being murdered by a fellow American.
5. The official Chinese News Agency, located in the city of Xinhua, estimates that there are ten million guitar players in their country today, an amazing number considering that the instrument was banned during the Cultural Revolution, which lasted ten years, from 1966 to 1976.
6. Two hundred thirty-one electoral votes were cast for James Monroe but only one for John Quincy Adams in the 1820 presidential race.
7. The British soldier T. E. Lawrence, better known as "Lawrence of Arabia," stood less than five feet, six inches tall.
8. Drinking a glass of French wine makes me giddy before my ten o'clock English class, held in Wrigley Field every other Friday, except on New Year's Day.
9. When a political opponent once called him "two-faced," President Lincoln retorted, "If I had another face, do you think I would wear this one?"
10. Alexander Graham Bell, inventor of the telephone, died in Nova Scotia on August 2, 1922; two days later, on the day of his burial, for one minute no telephone in North America was allowed to ring.

Part 5

Additional Readings

Chapter 23

Exposition: Development by Example
p. 579

■ **"Darkness at Noon" by Harold Krents—p. 579**

Questions on Content, Structure, and Style

1. What is Krents's thesis? Is it clearly stated?
2. How does Krents support his claims?
3. Of the examples presented, which is most effective? Why?
4. Which of Krents's examples is least effective? Explain.
5. Are there any points raised by Krents that would be strengthened by additional illustrative examples? Explain.
6. What is Krents's purpose in writing this essay? Who is his intended audience?
7. Describe Krents's tone (e.g., "at which point even my saint-like disposition deserted me").
8. What does Krents mean when he writes in his opening paragraph that he sees himself only in "the image I create in the eye of the observer. To date it has not been narcissistic"? Contrast this paragraph with his conclusion. Do they address the same issue? Why or why not?
9. How is Krents's essay organized? Does it follow a logical, effective order?
10. This essay was originally published in 1976. Is it still relevant today? Have Krents's hopes for the future come to pass? Cite examples to support your answer.

Answers to Questions

1. Krents's thesis is not overtly stated; instead, his claim that handicapped individuals are the victims of ignorance-based discrimination is implicit in the essay.
2. The author's claim is supported with several personal experiences.
3. Students might argue that the hospital example, because of its vivid detail and dialogue use, is the most effective.
4. The example of being "turned down by over forty law firms" is perhaps less effective than the others since it is presented in such general terms. Krents notes that this "will always remain one of the most disillusioning experiences" of his life, yet it is not described in detail.
5. Showing one of the law firm rejections in detail, using dialogue and the same level of specific sensory detail as he did in the hospital example, would make Krents's description of this experience more powerful for the reader.
6. Krents's purpose in writing this essay, originally published for a general audience in *The New York Times,* is to show nonhandicapped readers how ignorance and misperceptions can lead to discrimination.
7. Krents uses a combination of humorous examples—to illustrate the ludicrous treatment of the handicapped—and honest, straightforward statements of frustration and hope to drive his points home.
8. The opening paragraph indicates that as he is blind, Krents "sees" himself as others see him, and because of public misperceptions it is not an overly flattering image. His concluding paragraphs imply that these misperceptions do not have to exist. Just as the young girl, in the innocence of childhood, does not recognize the handicap, so too can the plant manager learn to look beyond physical disabilities.
9. Krents's essay is organized logically by example, moving from instances where he experiences discrimination to experiences illustrating his hope that this discrimination will end.
10. Student responses to this question will vary, but all should be supported by examples. With fully developed examples, answers to this question could serve as the basis for student essays.

Vocabulary

1. narcissistic (1)—characterized by excessive love of self
2. enunciating (2)—pronouncing
3. conversely (2)—reciprocally, contrarily
4. graphically (5)—powerfully
5. disposition (13)—temperament
6. cum laude (15)—with distinction

■ "Black Men and Public Space" by Brent Staples—p. 581

Questions on Content, Structure, and Style

1. What effect on the reader does Staples intend with his opening line?
2. Does Staples use primarily hypothetical or specific examples as support? Why does he make that choice for this particular essay?

3. In paragraphs 6 and 7, the author tells of his boyhood in Chester, Pennsylvania. Why does he include this information?

4. Is Staples's thesis statement implicit or explicit? Write a thesis statement for this essay in your own words.

5. Staples includes an example in paragraph 10 of another black male journalist who experienced a similar negative reaction. Why does Staples include this example in addition to his own?

6. What are some of the more vivid details the author used to develop his examples? What is the impact of those details on the reader?

7. This essay was written in 1986. Do you believe these same experiences could happen today? In your community?

8. What prejudices have you experienced or witnessed? Besides race, what other stereotypes are held today and are causing people to be prejudged? Are stereotypes always negative?

9. In paragraph 5, Staples says "young black males are overrepresented among the perpetrators of that violence [toward women]." What does he mean? Why does he acknowledge that fact?

10. What is the tone of this essay? What evidence can you cite to support your answer? Does the conclusive paragraph provide evidence that Staples has adequately learned to deal with the problem, or is there evidence of some residual bitterness in the conclusion?

Answers to Questions

1. Staples intends to shock the reader to attention with this overstated, purposeful misrepresentation of his experience.

2. The specific, real examples are important in this essay because, without them, a reader might accuse Staples of whining or misinterpreting people's actions. When he provides exact incidences, the reader can see how often Staples actually was prejudged and understand how frustrating those experiences must have been for him.

3. Knowing that Staples was a "good kid" and that, while he saw violence in his home town, he was not part of it, is important for the reader in order to understand why he was so surprised at the reactions he received. Also, he was "scarcely noticeable" in his hometown in contrast to the constant awareness and suspicion he experienced in Chicago and New York.

4. The complexity of Staples's thesis is not explicitly stated in the essay, although a very concise summary of the topic appears in paragraph 11: "Over the years, I learned to smother the rage I felt at so often being taken for a criminal." A more complete thesis statement would include a clearer indication of his attitude toward these experiences: "After many negative experiences of being stereotyped as a potential criminal, I have unfortunately had to change my appearance and behavior to avoid being perceived as threatening because of my race."

5. Showing that other black males have the same experiences indicates the problem is larger than just his own and that he has not imagined or exaggerated his situation.

6. Staples describes himself ("a broad six feet two inches with a beard and billowing hair, both hands shoved into the pockets of a bulky military jacket") so that the reader can imagine the vision that threatened his "victim." The "thunk, thunk, thunk" of the door locks is also easy to imagine. The jewelry store owner ("her eyes bulging nearly out of her head") and her "enormous red Doberman pinscher straining at the end of a leash" help the reader picture the fear people feel when he confronts them.

7. Student responses will vary.

8. Students can relate to Staples's experience more closely when they discuss the types of stereotyping in which they have been involved. Teenagers certainly are stereotyped and others have instant stock reactions to them in many cases. They might also discuss religious and gender prejudices they have experienced.

9. Students often misread this statement. They often think Staples is saying that blacks are incorrectly suspected of being violent while he is actually conceding that more blacks than whites *are*, in fact, perpetrators of violence against women—he's just not one of them. This concession is important to show the reader that he is attempting to be very fair about his observations.

10. Student opinions will differ very strongly on this question. Some will believe Staples is comfortable with the adjustment he has made while others will see an underlying edge to his resignation with the system. Staples's tone is not lividly angry, but he is unhappy that his race has to live with and accommodate such prejudice.

Vocabulary

1. unwieldy (2)—hard to manage
2. dicey (2)—questionable
3. errant (2)—wandering from a regular course
4. taut (4)—tight, tense
5. warrenlike (5)—as a crowded group of buildings
6. solace (5)—consolation, comfort
7. perilous (8)—dangerous
8. ad hoc (8)—for this case only
9. skittish (11)—easily frightened
10. congenial (11)—friendly, compatible

■ "Why Don't We Complain?" by William F. Buckley, Jr.—p. 583

Questions on Content, Structure, and Style

1. What was your initial reaction to Buckley's title (prior to reading the essay)? Did it change after reading the piece?

2. What is Buckley's main idea? Is it also his thesis?

3. What do language choices such as "virile age" (2), "the gauntlet of eighty sweating American freemen" (3), "trooped out" (6), and "I would speak out like a man" (12) suggest about the narrator's attitude toward action? His values? Gender?

4. How does the first example of "not complaining" about the heat in the train function to unify the essay?

5. How do the succeeding examples up to paragraph 19 relate to the opening example and help to organize the text?

6. Where does Buckley diverge from providing yet another example and into opinion, and why?

Answers to Questions

1. Answers will vary. Is Buckley calling on us to make a complaint or is he going to tell us why we don't complain? His title sets up certain expectations in the reader that may seem to go unfulfilled. But a close reading should reveal that both expectations are fulfilled in that he encourages us to complain once he explains why we don't.

2. Buckley's main idea is that we don't complain when perhaps we ought to. His thesis is a bit less direct in that he sees the lack of complaining in the American public as an abdication of our will to self-determination (paragraphs 19 and 20). This is not just a matter of whining to have our needs and desires fulfilled on a day-to-day basis, but rather a matter of considering our collective existence and freedom. In a way, Buckley is referring to maintaining our freedom and our rights to it.

3. These language choices suggest a stereotypical view that action, in this case complaint, is the purview solely of men and that it must be accomplished authoritatively and with, perhaps, some violence. Such an attitude toward complaint suggests that Buckley is working within a dated cultural expectation of both men and women, and even of relations and negotiations. Knowing this may help to explain why so many are averse to making complaint. Still, Buckley does not reject the stereotypical view. He does, later, find a more articulate and less volatile response to his complaint when he begins to analyze the reasons for its skittish practice.

4. The example of the overheated train as metaphor of irony is that it is a vehicle of mass transport. It not only conveys, it contains and thus functions to help suppress the masses. The train represents the country itself, moving those within it toward passive acceptance of displeasure. There are layers of symbolism in this first example that students can explore further in an extended discussion.

5. The examples that follow the first include: 1) the out-of-focus movie theater picture, 2) the narrator's complaint that he can't complain, 3) the waitress's late delivery of milk with his breakfast, 4) the ski repair store incident wherein he needed a screwdriver, and 5) the airline attendant not retrieving his food tray so that he could reach under his seat for more paper. In the first example of the movie theater, Buckley shows how not one person in a large group complains even though all suffered, thus echoing the scene in the train. However, he explains that everyone most surely thought someone else would do the complaining, which is in juxtaposition to his aborted attempt on the train. In example 2, he bemoans his inability to complain and reverses the aborted attempt begun on the train by resolving to change his habits, which he fails to do in example 3. Still, the milk incident helps to further his resolve. He follows through in example 4 but is roundly repudiated in his effort when the shopkeeper is whisked away by the army and the remaining crowd resembles the dour train passenger whose "resentful stare" silenced our hero in the train example. The comedic effect of this scene draws our attention to Buckley's "recognition" that he has been "reversed." What's more is that the notion of "reversal" here—"I put the experience down as a reversal" (paragraph 17)—is entirely apropos to Buckley's intentions. *His* tragedy, however, is comical because it is set against the dramatic scene of a helicopter swooping in to rescue a man who had just had a heart attack and who sat unperturbed by it all. Example 5 continues the story. Our narrator/hero is less

than heroic in his sarcasm, which is the result of his previous encounters. He has fallen into pithy response to make himself feel better, rather than to accomplish change. In this scene, there is no attempt to reconsider. He has simply "run out of paper." He cannot even editorialize. His emasculation is complete.

6. The organizational strategy discussed above allows Buckley to shift gears in paragraph 19 to retrieve, or at least reestablish power (self-determination, masculinity, choose your metaphor) in a new way—via thoughtful analysis and careful discourse. His humiliation is ours, empathetically, and we can now listen, as the passenger in the train did not want to do, to our fellow passenger in life. We can listen to him consider a few ideas on how we became so passive ("read: apathy" paragraph 22) in our dealings with injustices, big and small. He believes that we must watch out, speak out, and re-establish our self-determination as a people, for as numbers increase toward apathy, Khrushchevian thinking has the potential to increase as well. While Buckley's argument may echo typical conservative thought in the political-rhetoric "wars," he presents it to the reader for debate in his final statement when he clearly notes that he has an opinion—"I may be crazy, but I say . . ." (paragraph 23). In doing so, he reclaims his right to complain and asserts his views in a responsible fashion—one that allows him expression without reprisal, except vis-à-vis the written word, and one that assures his fellow passengers in life that they, and he, needn't fear an over-zealous physical response.

Vocabulary

1. commutation (2)—substitution in a charge as in for payment or for criminal punishment
2. doleful (2)—without cheer; full of grief
3. sibilant (2)—containing the sound or letter of s as in "hiss"
4. stupor (2)—numbness or condition of amazement
5. gauntlet (3)—two rows of men facing each other with clubs or weapons intended to beat at an individual running between the rows
6. consigned (3)—to give over to another's custody or care; to relinquish one's position
7. supine (4)—lying on one's back; mental or moral lethargy
8. dissolution (4)—disintegration; decay
9. vexation (4)—state of being annoyed
10. hectoring (5)—bullying
11. purposive (7)—serving a useful end, though not necessarily one designed
12. intimated (9)—hinted at
13. complexus (9)—an interwoven, complicated combination of things
14. bellicose (9)—combative
15. Milquetoast (11)—comic strip character that represented a man afraid to assert himself (created by H.T. Webster)
16. ostentatiously (11)—with an overabundance of flair; showing off elaborately
17. centripetal (16)—moving toward the center; having a unifying effect
18. technification (19)—movement toward all things being complex, manufactured, or precise
19. plenipotentiary (21)—invested with full power
20. fascists (22)—those who subscribe to the principles of Fascism, which promotes a centralized autocratic national regime that exercises extreme regimentation of industry, commerce, finance, and communication.

Chapter 24

Exposition:
Process Analysis
p. 587

■ **"The Jeaning of America" by Carin C. Quinn—p. 587**

Questions on Content, Structure, and Style

1. Quinn maintains that jeans are a symbol of the American way of life. What do they symbolize?
2. What are the main stages or steps in this process analysis?
3. This essay follows the development of blue jeans to 1978, when it was written. What stages would you add to the process to bring it up to date?
4. What does the narrative of Strauss's life add to this process analysis?
5. What descriptive details add more interest to the process of the invention and development of blue jeans?
6. Why do you think Quinn has chosen this topic to research and write about? What is her audience and purpose?
7. Where do you see transitional devices used to tie pieces of the process together?
8. What strategy does Quinn use to develop the concluding paragraph?
9. Our American culture has been known as a "melting pot" of many other cultures, and everywhere we can find French, English, Spanish, and German influences, among various others. What other distinctly American institutions/practices/objects such as blue jeans can you think of?

10. What objects that are an accepted part of your life might be interesting to trace back to their origins?

Answers to Questions

1. Blue jeans symbolize equality, ruggedness, frontier spirit and innovation.

2. a. Strauss goes west with canvas because he cannot make a living with his brothers.
   b. Strauss encounters a miner who complains about wearing out his pants.
   c. Strauss makes the miner pants from his fabric and the miner is enthusiastic about them.
   d. Fabric is changed to serge de Nimes (denim) by accident.
   e. Rivets are added by Davis as a joke.
   f. Easterners discover jeans in the 1950s at dude ranches.
   g. Popularity explodes during WWII with factory workers.
   h. Jeans are made all over the world and sold in great numbers.

3. Students might mention that there are now a multitude of manufacturers, styles, and colors; that the jean "look" has come to jackets, skirts, shirts, and shorts; that they are never supposed to look new now, but stonewashed and worn; that a whole new fashion statement has developed with torn, frayed, patched, and bleach-spotted jeans; or that "vintage jeans" have become an international phenomenon.

4. Without Strauss's personal history, the analysis would be a dry listing of events and dates; his story humanizes the process. Students might be encouraged to personalize their essays with anecdotes when appropriate.

5. Descriptive details that enliven the process are specific names, particularly Alkalai Ike, hauling 180 pounds of goods door to door, the fabric names and derivation of the term "jeans," numbers of jeans sold, and many others.

6. Quinn could be sure, when she picked this topic, that a broad readership would take blue jeans for granted and might be intrigued by the interesting and quirky process by which they were created and developed. Her purpose is probably both informative and entertaining.

7. Since the essay is arranged temporally, transitions related to time are used throughout: for two years, when, by this time, each year, etc.

8. The conclusion is a paragraph developed by example.

9. There are many possibilities for response such as barbecuing, rodeo, hot dogs, and football.

10. Students will find many objects they take for granted but seldom do they know how the object came to exist: skis, sunglasses, CDs, computers, neckties, Stetsons or ball caps, pieces of sports equipment (e.g., the refinement of baseball bats), etc.

Vocabulary

1. ubiquitous (2)—seeming to be present everywhere
2. emigrated (3)—departed from a place or country
3. eke (3)—manage to make a living (or find a solution) with difficulty
4. beckoned (4)—called or summoned by a slight gesture
5. pacify (5)—to calm, make peaceful
6. prospered (6)—thrived, flourished

7. commodity (6)—an article bought or sold
8. proletarian (6)—working class
9. idiosyncratic (6)—having a peculiar personal mannerism

■ "Skiing Lessons: The Cold, Hard Facts" by Dave Barry—p. 589

Questions on Content, Structure, and Style

1. Is Barry's introduction useful? How so?
2. Who is Barry's audience? What indicates this to you?
3. Does Barry's advice cover all the "steps" required to learn how to ski? Why or why not?
4. What organizational devices/strategies does Barry use?
5. What is Barry's tone in paragraph 2? Can you find other instances of its use?
6. What is the effect of putting "hit the slopes" in quotation marks? Look at Barry's uses of quotation marks elsewhere in the text. Do the marks contribute anything to the author's meaning beyond the expected?
7. How does Barry's style and title reflect the purpose of his content?

Answers to Questions

1. Barry begins with a direct statement about family vacations and moves the reader immediately into his topic. He does so with a sense of humor, thus preparing us for what is to follow. He does not exactly reveal that he will be discussing the steps to skiing in the introduction, but he has given us a preview into the fact that he is not a skilled skier in the statement "potentially knocking down a tree with your face." Since Barry's humoristic style is of a type, he clues the reader into it immediately and thus provides us with an opening that allows us relax at his expense.
2. Barry's audience is clearly parents but could be anyone. However, while his details can be grasped by anyone, they become exceptionally humorous if one has skied before.
3. No. He generally discusses the costs, financial and physical, which are the main purposes of his essay.
4. Barry begins with planning and then moves to the ski lessons. But he proceeds through each in a series of steps related to each. Within this construct he also uses cause and effect—a "special outfit" will cost you plenty and make you look like a "Giant Radioactive Easter Bunny From Space," goggles will fog up and will potentially cause you to crash into a tree, boots will cut off your blood circulation, etc.
5. Barry's tone is sarcastic. Responses will vary.
6. Barry's use of quotation marks might first be observed as simply identifying a cliché. However, when the entire context of the dangers of skiing are brought to bear, his use can be seen as a matter of highlighting an unpleasant aspect of skiing. The statement "hit the slopes" echoes "knocking down a tree with your face." Likewise, "Gore-Tex" has a similar ring. Other uses highlight Barry's sarcasm.
7. Barry's style is to use sarcasm to make us laugh at social constructs and expectations. The lesson learned here is that skiing is an absurd activity that may be more entertaining and less costly to watch than to experience.

■ "Beauty and the Beef" by Joey Green—p. 591

Questions on Content, Structure, and Style

1. The opening paragraph contains some highly descriptive language that appeals to our senses. Identify these and equate them to the appropriate sense. What is the affect on you as a reader?
2. What is the purpose of the opening paragraph?
3. What purpose does the second paragraph serve?
4. What is a Madison Avenue branding iron and how does it play into Green's purpose?
5. Is Green's essay an informative or directional process essay? What is he describing?
6. Describe the steps taken by the stylist.
7. Find some figurative language that Green uses to describe the stylist. In what other ways does Green portray the stylist? What do these references reveal about the tone of the essay?
8. Note a few examples that detail other parts of the filming process. What do they reveal about advertising?
9. Find as many references to "fat" at you can. How does Green use these terms to affect our perception of beauty? Of beef?
10. Examine the final paragraph. Does it conclude the essay effectively? Why or why not?

Answers to Questions

1. The following descriptions entice our appetite and make us hungry, which is the intent of the advertising as well: "juicy hamburger patty"—taste; "handsomely branded"—vision; "sizzling and crackling"—hearing; "roaring flames"—vision and hearing; "tender juices sputtering"—vision and hearing; "magnificent slab of flame-broiled beef"—vision; "crisp iceberg lettuce"—touch; "succulent red tomatoes"—taste and vision; "tangy onions"—taste; "plump pickles"—vision and touch; "towering sesame-seed bun"—vision, touch, and taste.
2. The opening paragraph both entices our appetite and invites us to continue reading in much the same way advertising lures us to purchase.
3. The second paragraph establishes Green's thesis—"the Whopper needs a little help from makeup" or what you see on television may not be what you get. There is an additional implicit thesis about how staged beauty creates an expectation and helps shape our range of perception regarding not only food, but beauty in general.
4. Madison Avenue obviously refers to the street in New York that houses advertising businesses. Branding iron functions here as a pun on labels as well as a tool. Green's purpose is to make the reader aware of the tools advertisers use to manipulate us.
5. Green's essay is essentially informative. He is describing how to build a visually appetizing burger.
6. The stylist follows these steps: 1) branding, 2) touching up, 3) juicing, 4) building or "fronting the ingredients on the bun," and 5) crafting the bun itself.
7. Specific figurative language includes "prissy microsurgical nurse" and "lens grinder." Other references portray the stylist as a manicurist (10); an artist using a paintbrush (4); a cook, salting (4); and even a mechanic, perhaps, who uses "motor oil." There are a number of ways to combine these images, none of them very flattering. Thus the tone is a tad sarcastic.

8. Other parts of the filming process might include how the food is delivered for filming (3); when the crew arrives and what they do (4); who watches in the wings (5); the necessary equipment—conveyor belt broiler, small electric heater, Q-tips, brushes, tweezers, etc.; the time it takes to film versus actual seconds of footage shown and the technical difficulties that contribute to this; and what is done with the day's carnage—tossing it all in the garbage. Responses to the question of what this says about the industry will vary, but students should be able to agree that the process of creating advertising is time consuming and therefore expensive. It is also highly superficial or highly artistic, depending on one's perspective. There is an opportunity here for further discussion and writing.

9. These terms—"grease," "lubricating," "oil," "glistening," "shimmering," and "glycerine"—suggest two things: fat and slickness. Both terms can be explored symbolically in relation to what advertising promotes. Some fat is merely grease, which is the reality, and fat that lubes and glistens provides an avenue to sales. The gimmicks of advertisement are slick and the revenues fat, as well. Moreover, beauty that is applied rhetorically or physically has a higher value than that found naturally. This is true for beef as well. The metaphor might further extend to equate "beef beauty" to human beauty as one and the same in the world of marketing.

10. The final paragraph is effective as a vehicle to the idea of how, at the end of the day, beauty is realistically valued as merely a means to an end.

Vocabulary

1. prissy (5)—prim and precise
2. preternaturally (8)—as though existing outside of nature

Chapter 25

Exposition: Comparison/Contrast

p. 593

- ### "My Real Car" by Bailey White—p. 593

Questions on Content, Structure, and Style

1. In order to be worth a reader's time, a comparison/contrast essay must have a point—a reason for looking at similarities and differences. Why does White compare these two vehicles?
2. Why does White spend much more time describing her "real" car than the new one?
3. A good comparison/contrast discusses parallel points about "Subject A" and "Subject B." What are the points White examines relative to the two cars?
4. To what senses does White appeal in her description of the two vehicles?
5. Much of what White tells the reader about her "real" car involves inconvenience. Where do you see glimpses of her affection for the car, despite its problems?
6. After reading about the new car, what do you think Bailey White's attitude is toward it?
7. What encounters with cars like the "real" car have you had on the road? What new perspective on those encounters might this essay give you?
8. From the description of the old car, what do you assume about White's abilities and personality?
9. If you took White for a ride in your car, or your family car, what observations might she make about it?

10. What object have you replaced that had sentimental value? Why was the replacement either a satisfaction or a disappointment for you?

Answers to Questions

1. White believes there is a certain emotional and sentimental value in possessions that cannot be equaled or replaced by a newer substitute.
2. The value and long-term connection with which White regards the old car is more important to her than the rather emotionless and sterile quality of the new car.
3. White compares exterior appearance, starting procedure, interior and comfort, sound, and ride ("We floated down the road").
4. White appeals to four of the senses: sight, touch, hearing, smell.
5. As well as several other places, White's last paragraph shows her connection to the car, which she still enjoys; paragraph 8, "a little smell of me," also demonstrates her bond with the car.
6. White appears to appreciate the convenience and comfort of the new car, but doesn't have the affection for it that she will always have for the other automobile, which is full of memories.
7. Students' answers will vary; many may comment that they now understand there may be an interesting and clever person behind the wheel and that their stereotypes may be far from reality.
8. Again, students will have different ideas.
9. Student responses will vary.
10. Student responses will vary.

Vocabulary

1. odometer (5)—a mileage gauge
2. ominous (9)—threatening, sinister, menacing

■ "Say Farewell to Pin Curls" by Anna Quindlen—p. 595

Questions on Content, Structure, and Style

1. Identify the comparisons and contrasts in each of the paragraphs.
2. Overall, what is the main metaphor that Quindlen uses?
3. What stereotypes do the details of girdles and garter belts, deference and duty, permanent waves and teasing combs specifically suggest about a woman's role?
4. In paragraph four, Quindlen shifts her point of view from the child's to the parent's. Is this effective? Why or why not?
5. Is the method of comparison used in this essay effective? Why or why not?
6. What do the images "baby beauty queens" (3) and "throwing sons with pony tails out of the house" have in common?
7. Quindlen includes a rhetorical question at the end of paragraph four. Why? How does it add to our understanding her reasons for writing? What tone does it carry?
8. What do the details in paragraph three reveal about the narrator?
9. Why is the opening sentence so time specific?
10. Where is Quindlen's thesis? Is it implicit or explicit?

Answers to Questions

1. Comparisons include the following: in p.1—hair to surprised face, face to flat shade with ruffled curtains; p. 3—sleeping on curlers to having a shoebox for a pillow. She also contrasts looking normal to what she actually looks like in this paragraph, but it is indirect. We have in p. 4—cutting children's hair to warfare; p.5—barbershops to battle-grounds; p. 6—helmet-hair updos to hairstyles worn by brides and grandmothers; p. 7—humans to their roles, life for women to a masquerade, extroversion to mania, conventions for females to manic ringlets and freedom to long hair on boys; p.8—freedom to birthright, mohawk to cockscomb, tyranny of freedom to nonconformity and thus non-conformity to conformity, and finally, a tie to a noose.

2. "Hair wars" (8) is Quindlen's main metaphor for the tension played out between parents and children or teens.

3. Girdles and garter belts suggest chastity; deference and duty suggest obedience; and per-manent waves and teasing combs suggest beauty—each of which functions as a type of constraint. While Quindlen speaks of such constraints in relation to herself, she broad-ens the discussion to children in general by revealing her negotiations with her son. The question then becomes one of paternalism—at what point are children of either sex allowed to express themselves as they wish?

4. Yes, for it allows her to show how the taming of her hair had tamed her. This is impor-tant for the reader's understanding of how she came to be the "loosey-goosey" parent.

5. This essay seems to follow the point-by-point method more than the block method, but one could argue that the shift that occurs in paragraph 4 creates a block construction. Whether or not she is effective is debatable. Certainly her imagery creates interest and asks us to examine her overall meaning.

6. These images force us to look at gender roles as they are or have been defined socially, via culture and generation.

7. Quindlen reveals that she does not agree with dressing children as adults. She would rather treat them respectfully, allowing them to find their own boundaries and maturity. In some way maturity recognizes convention as part of negotiating life—i.e. her son agrees to buzz back his hair before prom and she does not interfere in her son's growth by forcing trivial issues and thus potential resentment that might delay real growth in human relations and knowledge of self. The tone is one of frustration and a bit of sar-casm in the line in question. But Quindlen is so certain of her position that the question itself functions as a retort that allows her to further her argument without rancor.

8. The details in paragraph three reveal the author's discomfort with her role as a child and as a female as defined by her mother and the church.

9. The timeline, Easter to June, is again referred to in paragraph three, which explains why the attention to her head is so important—there are many social events that fall during those months.

10. Quindlen has an explicit and simple thesis in the final sentence—"The hair wars are over." But her implicit thesis is that children should be given enough respect to make their own decisions and learn from them rather than having their behavior dictated.

Vocabulary

1. ebullient (2)—to bubble or boil out or over
2. overweening (4)—arrogant; egotistical; conceited

3. internecine (4)—mutually destructive slaughter
4. self-abnegation (6)—to deny to oneself or to restrain oneself
5. unfettered (7)—without restraint
6. girdles (7)—an undergarment that functioned to slim the waist, hips, and thighs
7. garter belts (7)—a device worn around the hips and waist to hold up nylon stockings
8. cockscomb (8)—the ruffle of feathers on top of a rooster's head
9. impromptu (8)—unplanned; spontaneous

■ "Once More to the Lake (August 1941)" by E.B. White—p. 596

Questions on Content, Structure, and Style

1. What contrasts are set up in the first paragraph? What language suggests this?
2. White uses several extended metaphors in this essay. What comparisons are made in paragraph 2?
3. What is the dominant impression in this essay?
4. Identify a few particularly strong images that contribute to the dominant impression.
5. Why does the narrator return to the lake? What does he expect to get from the trip?
6. While White's essay is primarily organized through comparison, what additional organizational strategies does he employ?
7. The narrator repeats the words *peace, goodness,* and *jollity* in paragraph 10, which he had previously used in paragraph 9. These keywords tie into the overall theme but because the word order shifts from one paragraph to the other, there seems to be a shifting in the theme as well. What other statements indicate that not all is as it once was?
8. Other than a nostalgic, descriptive narrative, what is White's purpose?
9. Why is the date (August 1941) in the title significant?
10. Paragraph 12 relates the events of a summer thunderstorm. If viewed as a metaphor, what possible meanings can be found in this passage that would lend greater meaning to the final sentence?

Answers to Questions

1. White contrasts noise and quiet, stress and relaxation, and the moods associated with times and places. Keywords that suggest these contrasts are found in the harsh descriptions of the ocean—"restlessness of the tides," "fearful cold of the sea water," and "incessant wind"—versus the soft qualities of the lake itself and the first memories he relates—"the placidity of the lake," "kittens," "Pond's Extract" (a bit of a pun), and even "ringworm," which, although not a pleasant thought, does have a certain edgeless feeling about it.
2. White compares the lake and the woods that surround it to a cathedral. More than that, however, is a comparison between the holiness of the place and family, for it is in the memory that he recalls the stillness and the respect not to disturb it or his family.
3. The dominant impression is one of a tranquil connection between the past and present.
4. Responses will vary but the majority of them ought to come from the five senses—"I felt the same damp moss . . . saw the dragonfly alight . . ." (5); "the first smell of the pine-laden air . . . no fuss, no loud wonderful fuss" (9).

5. The narrator returns presumably to relax, but there is an underlying element in his associations that clearly causes him to remember his father and so he may also be trying to determine what kind of relationship his father built with him. This aspect of the text is somewhat vague, however, and there is more emphasis on episodic scenes wherein memories intertwining with the present produce a focus on tranquil continuity.

6. Chronology primarily, which he uses to return the reader's orientation back to the present, is also interspersed with spatial description and descriptive episodes of memory.

7. Students will have many options here, but a few clearly indicate shifts in focus—"There had always been three tracks to choose from . . . ; now the choice was narrowed down to two" (7); "The waitresses were still fifteen; their hair had been washed, that was the only difference" (7); "The postcards that showed things looking a little better than they looked" (8), etc.

8. Again, responses will vary, but the strongest theme seems to be one of family and connections through time, the passing along of traditions both through the narrator and the narration itself. In paragraph 12 he notes a "joke about getting drenched linking the generations in a strong indestructible chain" and thus clues the reader to the cultural connections people share when they share experiences. He attempts to bridge time and place by keying into rural life and the idyllic. The story has a pastoral quality that establishes a mood of reflection early on and then sustains it till the very last line, which abruptly shifts the tone toward fear.

9. The year 1941 is significant in that it is the year the United States. officially entered World War II. It also marked the establishment of the Atlantic Charter, a document that linked the United States and Great Britain as having in common certain principles in their respective national policies. It also became the year of the great push toward hydroelectric power, which may not at first seem significant, but could be considered relevant if one views this tale through a historical lens. The United States had been providing goods and producing war materials for those countries already engaged in the war. Sustaining such massive production required great quantities of power, and a good many dams were built for this purpose. While White makes no mention of his memorable lake as a source of power, he does very clearly suggest a connection to technological progress in paragraph 10 with the noise and the prevalence of "outboard" motors. There are multiple other connotations in paragraph 10 relating to boys learning to control motors, which surely provide additional areas for discussion and which also add to the layers of meaning White so deftly weaves. In terms of historical significance, however, the title provides an avenue of discussion for viewing America, and perhaps the world, in those prewar days as though through "a dropped curtain" (7), as representing youthful innocence and idealism and idyllic splendor. Published in 1941, White's text is a piece of Americana, whether he intended it to be or not.

10. Paragraph 12 relates the events of a summer thunderstorm and in doing so suggests a multitude of meanings. The general stereotypical associations involve change, impending doom, death, rebirth, cycles, etc. White's treatment of it is such that it at first appears to be one more episode that harkens to the past and sustains tradition. As such it can simply be viewed as a change in the weather that adds to the connections of human existence. Yet, it is a key aspect that the storm occurs near the end of the tale and seems to become a precursor to the final statement: ". . . suddenly my groin felt the chill of death" (12). Responses will vary and should be encouraged through a writing assignment that allows them to explore more fully the richness of this essay.

Vocabulary

1. incessant (1)—nonstop
2. spinner (1)—a fishing lure
3. coves (2)—small secluded inlets or bays
4. tentatively (3)—subject to change or withdrawal
5. pensively (5)—thoughtfully
6. premonitory (12)—giving previous warning

Chapter 26

Exposition: Definition
p. 601

■ **"Celebrating Nerdiness" by Tom Rogers—p. 601**

Questions on Content, Structure, and Style

1. How does Rogers initially define a nerd?
2. Why does Rogers begin with the definition he does?
3. Who is the author's audience? How do you know?
4. What is the author's purpose? How can you tell?
5. How does Rogers want nerds to be viewed? (How does he redefine?)
6. What strategy does the author use in paragraph 3 to transition between the stereotypical definition and his own?
7. Identify some other strategies of definition on page **238—239** in your text that Rogers uses in his essay.
8. The tone in the essay shifts perceptibly throughout the essay. Compare a few paragraphs. Where is Rogers sarcastic? Humorous? Fatherly? Defensive? Can you find others?
9. Where is Rogers's thesis? Does its placement seem appropriate? Why?
10. In paragraphs 4 through 10, Rogers links his discussion and his paragraphs through an ongoing discussion of his children. How does he link paragraph 1 to paragraph 2? 2 to 3? 3 to 4?

Answers to Questions

1. Initially, Rogers uses the stereotype—"friendless, book-smart sissies who suck up to authority figures."

2. He provides a recognizable characterization to invite the reader in to compare and contrast the simplistic view with a personal one.

3. The author is writing both to other nerds and to the public. In general, he chooses to include himself in the category of nerd and identifies himself as a teacher, thus alerting the audience to his personal perspective and, perhaps, an intent to teach. But he uses the pronouns "we," "us," and "our," which allows nerds to identify and benefit from his celebration.

4. The author's purpose is to celebrate nerds. The title gives it away. However, he has the additional purpose of negating a negative stereotype in the process, thereby disempowering it and empowering those who have been labeled nerds.

5. He redefines nerds through a comparison to famous inventors considered geniuses and then relates the success of his own children, showing them to be courageous in the face of social rejection and bullying, well-traveled, and witty.

6. Rogers transitions between the stereotype and his own definition in paragraph 3 by comparing and contrasting—nerds, in the abstract, famous nerd geniuses, nerds known personally. The personal representation allows for sympathetic response not found in the stereotype.

7. Other strategies found involve a description of characteristics (1); definition by negation—not "suck-ups" (1); compares to geniuses (3); gives examples (2, 5, 6, 8, 9, 10); discusses causes and effects (throughout); identifies times and places of use (1, 2, 3, 4, 10); and associates the term with recognizable people throughout but perhaps most notably in paragraph 3 and whenever he mentions school and bullies.

8. Answers will vary.

9. The thesis is the last sentence. It is appropriate here as Rogers invites the reader to participate in reformulating his/her own view to his idea without his having to defend it.

10. In paragraph one, he introduces himself as a nerd; in paragraph two he shifts from awareness of the label to a recollection of when he came to understand the effect of the label. In paragraph three, he explains how one effect caused another—his becoming a teacher—and then discusses how teachers partake, like others, in rejecting nerdiness despite the fact that such behavior is antithetical to their purpose. He then moves from the geniuses as examples to equating them to teens in American high schools, which then allows him to discuss his children in paragraph four and the remainder of the essay.

Vocabulary

1. inane (1)—insignificant
2. virtually (3)—almost; not real
3. eccentric (3)—odd, deviant from the norm
4. arrogant (3)—having a feeling of superiority and showing it to others
5. transcribed (8)—to make a copy of through writing

■ "O the Porch" by Garrison Keillor—p. 603

Questions on Content, Structure, and Style

1. In his definition, Keillor defines what a *useful* porch isn't as well as what it is. What *isn't* a useful porch in his perspective?
2. At the end of paragraph nine, Keillor states that "a golden creamy silence suffuses this happy scene, and only on a porch is it possible." What does he mean?
3. Is Keillor's language elaborate or simple? What does it add to his thesis?
4. If, as the author notes, the porch is a place for the "company of pals" (8), why are passersby seemingly unwelcome (10)?
5. How does the terrace fit into Keillor's idea of what a porch should consist of?
6. What is the purpose of paragraph eight?
7. In paragraph four, he says a "good porch" lets you do a number of things without "having to run away from home." What does he mean?
8. In paragraph nine he states: "There, silence indicates boredom and unhappiness and hosts are quick to subdue it into speech." Subdue seems an odd word choice here. Why do you think he uses it?
9. What does the author mean in paragraph 11: ". . . we feel richer than Rockefeller and luckier than the President"? How are they richer and luckier?
10. What is the structural strategy presented at the outset of the essay?

Answers to Questions

1. What is not Keillor's idea of a useful porch is one that is "only a platform" (1), one that allows you to only greet people (2), one that is overly decorated as a house would be (8), and one that doesn't allow you to spill or be undecorated yourself.
2. He's referring to the difference between being outside and inside, being free to do what one pleases versus what one is expected to do. His is arguing that a porch contains family and friends, but it does not cage or restrain them. It is an extension of the home as a comfort zone.
3. Keillor's language is neither elaborate nor contrived. In paragraph nine he uses *me* in the subject position, thereby declaring freedom from conventions and social expectations, which is precisely his aim for porch discourse.
4. The porch is by invitation only, so that one can participate in "drinking orange pop from cans"—being casual and comfortable—while viewing the world go by. It allows one to feel like royalty without the expense. Keillor suggests that the decorum of porch sitting requires decorum from the public rather than the porch sitters. The effect is to define the boundaries of porches both physically and emotionally.
5. The 12th floor puts them far above the passersby, but with a view of rooftops, chimneys, treetops, and the street below they are both connected to the street and removed from it in much the same way a screened porch would function. The canopy, plants, and deck chairs provide a "balance between indoor and outdoor life" (3), thus affording them a sense of both privacy and simplicity.
6. Paragraph eight functions to move the text forward between the past and the present, between the values of yesteryear and their disappearing act in modern times. He makes us think about the value of the dollar against that of friends and family, and he encourages not only relaxation, but restoration.

7. Responses will vary, but students can be encouraged to view the idea of vacationing as a manner of "running away from home" to gain rest, escape everyday pressures, and avoid social obligations.

8. Again, answers will vary, but the word's connotation suggests an attempt to control, on the part of the hostess, which is quite the contrary to behavior on the porch. Thus, the theme of ease is further promoted.

9. They are rich in friends and lucky to have a porch to share easy conversation.

10. Here the author is paving the way for the reader to understand paragraph 11 while using imagery that both relates to his topic of porches and plays on the idea of structure itself—the porch as structure and theme has duality that when considered together lends additional support, no pun intended, to his ideas of protected space and the contrasts of position, both physical and social. It is an elaborate metaphor.

Vocabulary

1. portico (2)—a balcony or covered passageway with colonnades
2. potentates (2)—those with great power as in rulers, princes, or dictators
3. decorous (4)—characterized by conformity to convention or social standards
4. parlor (4)—a room used primarily for visitors, rather than daily family use
5. rostrum (11)—a raised platform that juts out, as a pulpit, over or above the floor for a speaker
6. dais (11)—a raised terrace used for speaking
7. parapet (11)—a wall raised higher than another to protect soldiers, as on a fort, or a raised edge on a stage to prevent one from falling off
8. stockade (11)—a protective grouping of timbers intended to provide a barrier

■ "What Is Poverty?" by Jo Goodwin Parker—p. 604

Questions on Content, Structure, and Style

1. Summarize, as concisely as possible, Parker's definition of poverty.
2. What techniques does the author use to develop her definition? Note those that are especially effective.
3. Note the structure of the essay, with many paragraphs beginning "Poverty is . . .". Why is this effective?
4. What is Parker's purpose? Describe her intended audience (referred to as "you" in the essay; see paragraph 12).
5. As the biographical sketch of Parker at the beginning of the essay notes, little is known about her, including whether she is, in fact, writing from personal experience or whether she is an observer, using first-person point of view for effect. Does her identity matter to you as a reader, affecting the impact of the essay? Explain.
6. Is Parker aware of people who would be unsympathetic to her claims? If so, how does she address these people and their beliefs in the essay?
7. What parts of Parker's definition would be strengthened by additional development? Explain.
8. Parker relies on personal (subjective) experience to present her definition. Is this sufficient to convince her readers? Explain.

9. Characterize Parker's tone. She asks the reader to "listen without pity," yet does her tone evoke pity, or is it her subject that raises pity in the audience?

10. Compare Parker's opening and closing paragraphs. What emotional effect does she hope to have on her audience?

Answers to Questions

1. Parker defines poverty by powerfully describing how the poor must live—an existence of deprivation, illness, filth, fear, shame, and despair.

2. Parker employs a wrenching first-person narrative style that refers directly to the reader ("you") to describe and define poverty. She offers extensive, blunt personal illustrations of the daily life of the desperately poor, a stark contrast to the lives of most of her readers.

3. This repeated phrase jolts the reader with its relentlessness: over and over the phrase introduces a new horror to the reader, just as the poor must face ceaseless devastation.

4. Parker's purpose is to graphically reveal the true nature of poverty rather than offer a sanitized sociological definition. Her intended audience is those who have never known poverty and perhaps blame the poor for their condition.

5. Student responses to this question will vary; positions should be well explained.

6. Parker directly addresses individuals who are unsympathetic to the poor. Examples include paragraph 4 where she responds to the statement "Anybody can be clean." In paragraph 11 she notes, "But you say to me, there are schools." In both cases Parker answers the beliefs of these critics with her own experience.

7. Among the points that students might indicate need further development are those raised in paragraph 10 (children isolated from their peers by poverty; how poverty tempts children toward crime, drugs, and alcohol). Additional development might underscore the cyclical nature of poverty that Parker implies.

8. Parker does not pretend to offer anything more than her own experience to her readers so this narrative emerges as a powerful personal statement. While the addition of outside evidence would broaden Parker's base of support, it might also diminish the raw strength of the essay.

9. While readers may find that they do feel pity for the situation Parker describes, the description itself is not maudlin or filled with pathos. Instead, it is brutally direct and unflinching.

10. The opening and closing paragraphs of the essay highlight Parker's desire to move her reader to anger and action rather than passive sympathy.

Vocabulary

1. privy (2)—latrine, outhouse
2. chronic (3)—of a long duration or frequent recurrence
3. oleo (4)—margarine
4. pinkeye (11)—highly contagious eye infection

Chapter 27

Exposition: Division/Classification
p. 609

■ **"Party Manners" by Richard Grossman—p. 609**

Questions on Content, Structure, and Style

1. What is Grossman's thesis in this essay?
2. What reaction do you think Grossman wants from his readers?
3. Are Grossman's categories distinct or are they overlapping and ambiguous?
4. Is there a natural order to these categories? Why might the author have picked this order of presentation?
5. As you read, you probably thought of people you know and specific experiences you have had. What could Grossman have done to make his categories even easier to picture?
6. The author is a medical professional. Does it surprise you that the director of a New York medical center would write like this? Grossman's tone and style in this essay are undoubtedly different from the writing voice he would use for an article for a medical journal. What does this tell you about his writing ability?
7. What does Grossman think of the typical party? What kind of a party do you suppose Grossman would really like?

8. Grossman says this party behavior results, in large part, from nervousness and being ill at ease in a social context. What do you do when you are socially uncomfortable?
9. What acquaintances do you have who fit into some of these categories?
10. What is a character type that Grossman left out, but you see frequently at parties?

Answers to Questions

1. Many people use a party as a medium for acting out their deficiencies or unresolved problems.
2. Students will have different ideas. Grossman probably wants readers to identify with their party experiences and see these types as legitimate, but he may also want readers to reflect on their own behavior and try to enjoy the "warmth and closeness of other human beings" (9) instead of acting out.
3. Yes, the categories are quite distinct.
4. No strong natural order is evident, but Grossman may have picked the more neurotic types for the end in order to build up more clearly to his conclusion.
5. Students will give examples from their own experience; examples would enliven and validate Grossman's categories.
6. Competent writers are flexible; they can adjust their style, language, and tone to the purpose and audience they are addressing.
7. The author thinks the typical party is a psychologist's dream. He feels that party behavior is fake and neurotic. He might enjoy a party composed of good friends who could be totally natural with each other or a party organized around a topic or cause that would keep people from their "pathologic" behavior.
8. Students will give examples from their own experience.
9. Students will give examples from their own experience.
10. Suggestions will vary.

Vocabulary

1. promenades (1)—public places for walking
2. ubiquitous (2)—seeming to be present everywhere
3. foibles (3)—small moral weaknesses
4. martyred (6)—having chosen to suffer
5. rueful (6)—causing sorrow or pity
6. haranguing (7)—giving a long, blustering, and pompous speech
7. cryptic (8)—having a hidden meaning

■ "The Extendable Fork" by Calvin Trillin—p. 612

Questions on Content, Structure, and Style

1. Clearly Trillin is categorizing people who finish eating food on other people's plates. He neglects to categorize himself, however, claiming he is all four. Does he prove this? Do you believe him? If you had to name a category for him, what would it be?
2. Is there any division going on here?
3. What is Trillin's organization strategy for paragraphs one through five? Six through nine?
4. Where do you find hyperbole in this essay? What effect does it have on you?

5. Where might you "hear" a story like this? Does it sound familiar? What does it reveal about Trillin's purpose?
6. Why do you think "Alan's X-Tenda Fork" is evocative to Trillin?

Answers to Questions

1. He never really mentions himself except in relation to his wife and then only as a sampler, which should put him in the researcher category, but Sampler might be a more effective title. Responses will vary.
2. Trillin divides those whose plates are robbed into camps of those who allow it and those who don't. He also divides tasters into those who need an extendable fork and those who don't.
3. In the first paragraphs the category definitions carry the text. Beyond paragraph five Trillin's text becomes more complex. He has set up the reader for a discussion and now has to deliver. His wife provides a counterpoint to the initial implication that people don't want their plates raided. He in turn becomes identified as one who doesn't care, at least in relation to chicken. Then the fork returns as a topic, but the focus is on Alan as a sixth type of sampler—a glutton. Paragraph nine, however extends Alan's reach and his persona to bring the text back around to the "Finisher's" statement and thus the "finishing" of the essay.
4. Hyperbole is sprinkled throughout. A few include "the chicken looks as if it had been staked out on an anthill by a tribe of crazed chicken torturers" (7), "his tiny eyes dart from plate to plate . . . with a fork as quick as the strike of an adder (8), and "a sort of vacuum tube . . . install a tiny tape recorder . . ." and these all have visual humor. The latter also has sound as part of the humorist's attempt to capture our senses, because stealing food, in and of itself, isn't really funny. However, responses will vary.
5. Students should recognize a comedy club routine here. Obviously, entertainment through humor is the purpose, not categorizing.
6. The title is evocative because it creates a persona that the author can develop as a humorous device. A more utilitarian label for the fork would not excite the imagination quite as fruitfully. We can see how marketing and titles can pull us into a purchase or an essay.

Vocabulary

1. urchin (4)—a mischievous boy
2. subterfuge (6)—a deception made strategic and used to save face or avoid detection
3. adder (8)—a type of snake

■ "College Pressures" by William Zinsser—p. 613

Questions on Content, Structure, and Style

1. Is Zinsser's introduction too long? Is the length justifiable?
2. Is Zinsser's use of the first person (the "I") appropriate? Why or why not?
3. What general classes of college pressures does Zinsser cite?
4. Are the transitions at paragraphs 22 and 31 effective?

5. Evaluate Zinsser's language. Is the vocabulary level appropriate?
6. Characterize the tone of the essay. Is it formal? Informal?
7. Is Zinsser's use of dialogue and anecdotes to illustrate his points effective?
8. Which of the four pressures Zinsser discusses could students most easily relieve? How?
9. Zinsser cites four main pressures but discusses a fifth in some detail. What is it?
10. Does Zinsser's conclusion detract from the impact of his essay? That is, when he begins to show how many other interests students have, how they may not be as "obsessed" as he has portrayed them, does that lessen the meaning of his message?

Answers to Questions

1. The introduction is long—some 14 paragraphs. However, given the nature of the essay, and its tone and overall length, the long introduction seems entirely appropriate.
2. Although the first person can sometimes be a shortcoming in certain types of essays, making the thesis seem merely subjective, here it works well. Zinsser is an authority on his subject. Too, his audience—presumably his academic colleagues—would likely find his firsthand knowledge and "voice" appealing, if not necessary.
3. Economic, parental, peer, and self-induced.
4. The transition at paragraph 22 seems rather stilted, rather contrived. Consequently, the transition at paragraph 31, which is parallel to the one at paragraph 22, also seems rough.
5. Although Zinsser does not use particularly esoteric language or inflated diction, the reader needs to be well educated, or at least well read, to easily comprehend the author's meaning. The vocabulary level is rather high, but given the probable audience, fitting.
6. Despite some of the language used in the essay, the tone is quite informal, almost conversational.
7. In short, yes. A good rule of thumb for writers is to offer at least one concrete example for every abstraction. Zinsser's "stories," as he points out, are almost funny but not entirely because they illustrate the symptoms of a serious problem. However, the anecdotes, and the dialogue, tend to make what could have been a dry, formal, abstract essay both engaging and penetrating.
8. Obviously, the self-inflicted pressure. However, one could argue, as Zinsser does, that "it will be the students' own business to break the circles in which they are trapped"—including pressures placed on them by economics, parents, and peers.
9. Though Zinsser does not specifically include it in his four pressures, a fifth would be the pressures placed on students by professors.
10. On the contrary, the conclusion seems to effectively underscore his point. The last few paragraphs—though they to some extent are simple qualifiers—suggest that the problem, though real, can be remedied.

Vocabulary

1. supplicants (9)—those who ask humbly or earnestly, as in prayer
2. balm (9)—something that soothes or comforts
3. matriculates (17)—enrolls
4. tenacity (23)—persistence, stubbornness
5. pauperism (38)—poverty, beggary
6. blithe (46)—cheerful, carefree
7. codified (47)—arranged systematically, as laws
8. circuitous (48)—roundabout

Chapter 28

Exposition:
Causal Analysis
p. 619

■ **"The Teacher Who Changed My Life" by Nicholas Gage—p. 619**

Questions on Content, Structure, and Style

1. What is Gage's stated purpose in writing this essay? Are there other purposes as well?
2. According to Gage, what was Miss Hurd's greatest gift to him? What cause and effect relationship does this essay explore?
3. Gage's essay covers many years—nearly his lifetime, in fact. Why is this broad span of time important to his message?
4. What key scene best captures the essence of Gage's regard for Miss Hurd and her effect on his life? Explain your choice.
5. Are there any details given that are not vital to the central idea of the essay? Explain your selections.
6. Often, a key component of causal analysis essays is description. Choose two examples of effective description and indicate two sections of the essay in which the reader might want more descriptive detail.
7. There are two key uses of dialogue in this essay. Find these sections and explain why Gage may have chosen to emphasize these particular moments, rather than others, with dialogue.
8. Consider Gage's use of transitions between paragraphs, listing examples of smooth transitions and noting those that are more abrupt.

9. The success of an essay can be judged by its impact on its readers. What specific audience would benefit from Gage's piece? Why?

10. Gage uses several examples of Miss Hurd's behavior to illustrate her character. What traits emerge in the following paragraphs: 6, 8, 11, 15, 16, 17, 18, and 22? Why is this a more effective way of revealing her character to the reader than simply telling the audience what she was like?

Answers to Questions

1. Gage concludes his essay by stating that it is a tribute to Marjorie Hurd, but his larger purpose is to tell a broad audience how a teacher can make a dramatic difference in someone's life.

2. Her greatest gift to Gage was "direct[ing] [his] grief and pain into writing," giving him a new interest that was to change his life and goals. Miss Hurd (the cause) inspired him to hone his writing skills (effect) and steered him toward writing about his family (effect), which led to Gage's career as a writer and journalist (effect).

3. Gage's goal is to show how Miss Hurd changed his life and this can only be accomplished if readers are allowed to see her continuing influence on him as he matures personally and professionally.

4. There are a number of possible answers to this question but because of its detail and emotional impact, the most likely choice is the portion presented in paragraphs 8–12 where Gage discusses writing about leaving Greece. Readers are allowed to see through Gage's eyes how Miss Hurd's prompting had a powerful impact on him.

5. Here, too, answers will vary. Some students might feel that the details of family celebrations are irrelevant (the music, the food, the dancing) while others might argue that all of Gage's descriptions are appropriate to the focus of his essay. Debate on this subject will help students clarify their own views of the relationship between essay focus and development.

6. Student responses will vary.

7. Gage uses dialogue twice: when he first introduces Miss Hurd (this allows his readers to "hear" her just as he did, making her real to his audience) and when Miss Hurd calls after President Reagan's mention of Gage's mother (here she is seen as caring and warm, a contrast to her earlier words that round out his characterization of her).

8. There are any number of smooth, effective transitions that students might cite. Some more abrupt shifts include the transition between paragraphs 14 and 15 as well as 16 and 17, and 20 and 21.

9. No one answer to this question is "right." Students might argue that would-be teachers and writers would particularly benefit from reading the essay.

10. Paragraph 6 reveals her toughness, paragraph 8 her insight, paragraph 11 her pride and kindness; paragraph 15 shows her devotion, paragraph 16 her persistence, paragraphs 17 and 18 her compassion and thoughtfulness, paragraph 22 her deep regard for Gage. If Gage had told his readers she possessed these traits, rather than showing Miss Hurd in action, her portrait would not be as vivid.

Vocabulary

1. refugee (1)—displaced person
2. portly (2)—plump

3. layabouts (6)—lazy people
4. honed (7)—sharpened
5. Iron Curtain (9)—political and ideological barrier isolating an area
6. mortified (11)—humiliated
7. balky (16)—hesitant, uncooperative
8. serpentine (19)—snakelike
9. void (20)—emptiness
10. bounty (21)—abundance, plenty
11. testament (21)—tribute
12. catalyst (21)—agent causing an action
13. emphatically (21)—strongly, vehemently
14. eulogy (22)—informal statement of tribute to someone delivered after his or her death

■ "Spudding Out" by Barbara Ehrenreich—p. 623

Questions on Content, Structure, and Style

1. Who are the "salt of the earth," "silent majority," "viewing public," and "couch potatoes" in society?
2. Find a few examples of sarcasm within Ehrenreich's text. How does sarcasm assist her to make her point?
3. The author suggests several causes for "spudding out." Where do we find the ultimate cause of TV viewing?
4. Can you think of reasons for "spudding out" suggested by Ehrenreich's argument that discount TV as the primary cause?
5. How are Disney World and miniature golf related to the author's purpose?
6. Figurative language can help glue a text together via the extended metaphor. Find as many references as you can for TV viewers and results of viewing.
7. Has anyone you've known ever been "buried in a pothole" or "hurled from a collapsing bridge"? What effect do these statements have on the focus of this paragraph?
8. Where do you find hyperbole? What does it contribute to the reader's understanding of the author's meaning?
9. How does the artist Andy Warhol mentioned in paragraph nine fit into Ehrenreich's argument?
10. How many hours of TV do you view? What effect does it have on your life?

Answers to Questions

1. These terms refer to working class families who look to TV to provide cheap entertainment,
2. Answers will vary and there are many, such as "sapped and spineless" (1), "shut down the neighbor's pacemaker" (2), "virtues in mass agoraphobia" (3), and so on. Sarcasm functions here to bring humor to the piece so as to divert attention from any serious discussion of the medium's ill effects, which mimics her thesis that television detracts from thought, discussion and human interaction.

3. Ehrenreich saves the ludicrous for last in paragraph 10 where she claims that our love of TV viewing stems from not having to watch others watch TV—because that would be boring. Her previous claim in paragraph five was that our desire to have lives like those portrayed on TV because our own are so boring feeds into this cause. We could argue that the comparison of our lives to those on television creates the boredom with our reality, which would be admitting that television is both the cause of our boredom and our solution to it.

4. Ehrenreich attributes our boring lives to television viewing. Because we watch TV we have little interaction with others or the world, and so we want to watch TV. This is circular logic and she even alludes to it in paragraph five, referring to TV watching as way to escape reality—"The reason lies in an odd circular dynamic." The argument begs for a reason to turn on the tube in the first place—things like being too tired after work to do much of anything, not having money enough for other forms of entertainment, shifts in social dynamics, etc. In other words, the causes for "spudding out" may have less to do with television and more to do with social and industrial changes.

5. Disney World and miniature golf limit our view of outdoor leisure activities available to us. They are 20th century activities that require little thought, much in the way TV viewing asks little of us. But they are not overly active either.

6. Students should find these references to TV viewers or viewing: "salt of the earth," "silent majority," "viewing public," "couch potatoes" (1); "spud out," "Couch Potato Bags" (2); "spudhood" (7); "root vegetables" (8); "modern people, i.e., couch potatoes" (9); and "spuds" (10).

7. Hopefully, no one will answer in the affirmative and discussion can revolve around the idea that hyperbole is part of the author's sarcastic tone and attitude toward serious attempts (as in psychologists') to reason why people watch TV.

8. Hyperbole can be found in nearly every paragraph. It allows us to accept her illogical conclusion because we understand the entertainment value of her attempt to make us laugh at ourselves. At the same time, she mimics the "overdosing" quality of TV programming. We come not to care that her reasoning is faulty and choose simply to be entertained.

9. Warhol's art was considered by some to have little value beyond commercialism. However, Ehrenreich is clearly referring to what she considers his boring content of everyday items repeated in sequences. (There is an opportunity here for discussion of what art is and how it is valued, and for some research.) Viewing Warhol's work, in Ehrenreich's scheme, is equivalent to realizing one wants to "get up and make ice cubes" (7).

10. Responses will vary.

Vocabulary

1. agoraphobia (3)—fear of being in open spaces
2. infrastructure (4)—the basic system that underlies an organization or society, as in railways, waterways, roads, bridges, etc.
3. insipid (6)—lacking in interesting qualities
4. cathexis (7)—investment of emotional or psychic energy into a person, thing, or activity
5. bickering (9)—ongoing annoyances, argument, or nitpicking with another

■ "You Call This Progress?" by Seth Shostak—p. 624

Questions on Content, Structure, and Style

1. What does Shostak mean in paragraph 2 by e-mail "masquerading as a better way to put everyone in touch . . ."?
2. What is Shostak's thesis? Where is it stated?
3. In paragraph 2, Shostak adds a quip—"faster than you can say QWERTY"—to a sentence that otherwise is perfectly clear. Speculate on his reasons for doing so. How does it add to or detract from your understanding?
4. What assumption about work does Shostak hold as truth? How does this belief support his viewpoint?
5. Do you agree or disagree with Shostak's position?
6. To whom is Shostak writing? How can you tell?
7. What wording or punctuation suggests cause and effect relationships within the essay?
8. While the overall cause discussed is e-mail, what other results of its use lead to other effects?
9. What is Shostak's tone? How does it affect your interpretation of his argument?
10. Does his final assessment of the effects of e-mail in paragraph 9 seem logical to you?

Answers to Questions

1. Shostak argues that e-mail is a pretense for communication as it removes the receiver from the equation when it can be sent to a mailbox that no one actually needs to open. Literally, people neither talk nor "touch" each other and while a reply might be expected, it is often unnecessary.
2. The thesis can be seen best in paragraph 2—". . . e-mail has become an incessant distraction, a non-stop obligation and a sure source of stress and anxiety"—as these are points he argues throughout his essay.
3. Answers will vary, but some information about this quip is necessary. QWERTY equals the first six letters on the upper left side of a standard computer keyboard. This keyboard arrangement was devised to keep typists from typing faster than the old-style typewriter could function so as to avoid jamming the keys. The QWERTY keyboard signifies, in the context of this essay, a slower time. It lends both humor and purpose—Shostak wants to "slow down" or curtail the influx of e-mail that he must deal with.
4. Shostak believes work should produce something other than communiqués about work. Most likely, he sees a product or service as the result of labor, rather than talk, chat, or even memos.
5. Answers will vary, but discussion about the "information age" should prove revealing for the purpose of further thought about writing and its relation to subject-matter knowledge, which society prizes in education, and to work in the world beyond the classroom.
6. Shostak is writing to members of his own age group who are well educated. His elevated language and references to things like "old-style communication" (4), "Johnny can't read" (5), "carbon paper," and "brooms unleashed by the sorcerer's apprentice" (6) reveal his faith that readers will share his perspective.

7. Words and phrasing that suggest cause and effect include the following, but students may find others.

> result (2)
> Because (4)
> assumption is (4)
> usually produces (4)
> makes me yearn (4)
> Today, however . . . (4)
> byproduct (5)
> reason (5)
> because (5)
> It is not these. . . . Rather, it's . . . (6)
> Because (7)
> So . . . (7)
> Either way . . . (7)
> : [because] (7)
> If . . . , then . . . (8)
> Since (8)

8. Here are some possible responses:

Result	Effect
faster correspondence	more e-mail
more and more e-mail	consumption of time responding
	less time for work
	stress
instantaneous delivery	lack of patience for a reply
lack of patience	lack of politeness
	"knee-jerk" responses instead of thoughtful replies
relative anonymity	people who wouldn't normally write do, and do so poorly

9. Whiney, sarcastic, but humorous. Shostak's tone allows us to overlook his exaggerated claims to the destruction of civilization, while making us think about the role and impact of technology in our lives.

10. No, his final assessment is not logical, but some may think so. If this essay were evaluated as an argument it would fail the slippery slope test, but there is much here to suggest that the extremes Shostak presents are simply designed to grab our interest and reflect his level of frustration, which is readily acceptable as a logical result.

Vocabulary

1. ubiquitous (1)—capable of being everywhere
2. pernicious (1)—deadly
3. miasma (1)—an odorous vapor or fog once thought to cause disease
4. addled (1)—confused

5. QWERTY (2)—the upper left letters on a keyboard
6. convoluted (5)—complicated, coiled
7. ASCII (5)—American Standard Code for Information Interchange—a code used in computer science
8. proliferation (6)—rapid and repeated growth
9. deluge (7)—flood
10. Luddites (8)—a group of English workmen who destroyed labor-saving machinery

Chapter 29

Argumentation

p. 627

▪ A Scientist: "I Am the Enemy" by Ron Kline—p. 627

Questions on Content, Structure, and Style

1. Why does Kline begin with the first, provocative line?
2. What is the author's thesis regarding the use of laboratory animals?
3. What examples of medical advances from animal research does Kline offer as evidence to support this thesis?
4. Why does Kline refer to several major arguments frequently used against animal experimentation? What is the main reason he disagrees with anti-experimentation activists?
5. How does Kline refute the argument that computer simulation is a legitimate alternative to experimentation?
6. How does the author use emotional appeals? Are they effective?
7. What concessions does the author make to show he does understand that activists have sometimes had legitimate concerns?
8. Describe Kline's tone. How does he gain the confidence of a skeptical reader?
9. Kline claims that a "vocal but misdirected minority" has had too much influence on politicians and legislation. Do you agree with his assessment? What is the majority opinion? What current issues are often influenced by the strong voices of minorities? What historical issues have been subject to the strong influence of a minority? Is it good or bad that minorities can have such impact?

10. Is Kline's overall argument convincing? How could you make it more so? How might you argue against the essay?

Answers to Questions

1. Kline's blunt statement identifying himself as the enemy and the explanation of why he devotes his professional life to research personalize the opposition. Animal rights activists might find a villainous, heartless opponent more to their liking because it is much easier to demonize a vicious enemy. Kline's opening takes the fire out of that type of illogical and personal attack, and he turns the argument toward the reasonable purposes for using animals in the laboratory.

2. Kline believes animal research is essential to the continued development of new therapies and innovative surgeries. He criticizes both the public and his peers involved in medical research for not defending what he believes is a legitimate and ethical practice.

3. In paragraph 7, Kline explains that vaccines, antibiotics, drugs, and advanced surgical procedures have been developed with animal research. (Students should be asked if these are specific or hypothetical. How do they know? How could Kline make these examples far more convincing?)

4. When he acknowledges the major arguments of those opposed to animal research, he shows an understanding of their viewpoint. By doing so, he has the opportunity to explain why those viewpoints are not correct. His major point for his side of the argument is that human lives can be saved, and human pain and suffering can be diminished with the technology and other medical knowledge from continued experimentation on animals. He believes this probable outcome is a higher value than any suffering inflicted on the animals.

5. He explains that computer-simulated models cannot be as productive in medical research as they are in other sciences because of the inexactness of medicine and the complexity of biological systems.

6. Kline uses emotional appeals effectively to encourage the reader to apply the same kind of sympathy they might have for research animals to human beings in tragic medical circumstances. At the beginning of the essay, he compels the reader to see him as a humane researcher motivated by his concern for "healthy, happy children." In paragraph 3, he argues that those on his side of the argument might have allied the public more closely had they resorted to the same types of emotional appeals as animal activists by "waving equally sad posters of children dying of leukemia or cystic fibrosis." The next paragraph cites other examples of children in tragic accidents; using children rather than the elderly with Parkinson's, for example, is calculated to pull at the reader's emotions. As he concludes (paragraph 8), he once more reminds readers that his opinions come from his watching "many children die, and their parents grieve," and charges them to have as much compassion for dying humans as they would for a dog or cat.

7. In paragraph 5, Kline does agree that computer simulation has some value, principally to offer technological models. In his concluding paragraph, he admits that activists have improved conditions for experimental animals and that they have encouraged scientists to use suitable alternatives.

8. Throughout the essay, Kline's tone is reasonable and nonthreatening. He shows respect for his opposition rather than attempting to ridicule them; he gives activists credit in his conclusion for bringing attention to the humane treatment of animals involved in research.

9. Student responses will vary.

10. Students might add more detailed evidence of the many treatments and therapies that have been developed by using animal research, and evidence to substantiate that animals are indeed treated humanely in laboratory experiments. Those arguing against the essay might be reminded to maintain the reasonableness of their arguments, as has Kline, rather than resorting to purely emotional arguments.

Vocabulary

1. vilified (1)—made evil or sinful
2. inhumane (1)—cruel, brutal
3. simulation (2)—imitation, false resemblance
4. apathetic (2)—unfeeling
5. unconscionably (3)—unreasonably
6. malevolent (4)—wishing evil to others
7. placate (6)—to quiet or soothe anger

■ "Rethinking the Voting Age" by Ellen Goodman—p. 629

Questions on Content, Structure, and Style

1. What part of Vasconcello's bill to lower the voting age does Goodman reject? Is this a good reason for rejection?
2. In paragraph three, Goodman asks, "When should young people get to vote and why?" Does she ever answer this?
3. Note the author's use of the word "drive" in paragraph 11. How does this relate to Hanrara's metaphor in paragraph six?
4. Goodman's third paragraph alters the focus of the argument from what to what? Why does she do this?
5. Does paragraph four contribute to the essay? How?
6. What are the functions of paragraphs five through eight?
7. Does the reference to "training wheels" in paragraph nine affect Goodman's argument? How?
8. How would you identify this argument pattern?
9. Compare the tone of this essay to that of Ehrenreich's on page 579. How do they differ? Which do you find more reasonable? Convincing?
10. Do you think lowering the voting age will encourage civic participation and growth?

Answers to Questions

1. Goodman objects to fractionalizing teen votes, comparing it to when slaves were only considered three-fifths human, and thus suggesting that the bill would subjugate teens to similar legal status. She gives no reason why this would be offensive, but expects her reader to understand inequality as both a moral and Constitutional issue.
2. She hedges with a "if-we-do-this-we-should-do-it-this-way" approach in paragraph 10. She has re-framed the question to be "How do we get 18–25 year olds to vote?"
3. The metaphor likens voting to driving, or steering, to be more precise. In paragraph six she clearly states that she fears sharing the road with teens, but acknowledges that driving and voting may not be as alike as some have asserted and begins to address maturity

issues. In paragraph 11, she seems to be suggesting that older voters need a reason to vote, as much as youth do, and that teens may provide that impetus for those who fear their (teens') decision-making, or steering, skills. She could also mean that the population is aging and will literally require being transported to the voting booth. But because she has reiterated Hanrara's metaphor this is less likely.

4. Goodman wants to shift the emphasis to a more acceptable and reasonable discussion.
5. Paragraph four functions in the following ways: First, it provides a contrast in social responsibility and activity between the 1970s and current times, thus alerting the reader to an updated argument. Second, it suggests there has been little effort from youth in relation to voting, thus suggesting there is no need to revisit the issue of age. This then provides her with fodder for a discussion of, or allusion to, voter apathy, which she uses later.
6. Paragraph five focuses on the idea of coming of age, showing us that it can happen at various stages of life. Paragraph six shows the focus of pro-pre-teen voters and a typical paternalistic response. Paragraph seven summarizes the anti-pre-teen voter response and criticizes it, relying on paragraph five. Paragraph eight then shifts the argument back up to emphasize paragraph four's focus on the need for voters to vote, and de-emphasize the age at which they can.
7. The "training wheels" reference shifts the discussion back to the original discussion, tying again into the driving metaphor. However, now there is a focus on how to "better lower the voting age," which reminds us that the bill in California's legislature is not one the author wants to see passed without critical revision.
8. This is a Rogerian argument. It proposes a solution to an issue that the writer re-frames for more tolerable discussion.
9. It attains a reasonable tone with touches of humor. There is some reprimand, but it lacks the sarcasm of Ehrenreich's causal analysis. It is also much more thoughtful.
10. Responses will vary.

Vocabulary

1. anarchist (3)—one opposed to all forms of government
2. nascent (4)—beginning to exist
3. continuum (6)—something that is continuous and has no discernable variation except by reference to something outside of itself—i.e., time or space

■ "Judging by the Cover" by Bonny Gainley—p. 630

Questions on Content, Structure, and Style

1. What is Gainley's thesis? Where is it located? Is this an appropriate place for it? Why?
2. On what premises does Gainley build her essay?
3. Where does Gainley address the opposition?
4. To what does the author appeal in her argument?
5. What assumptions does Gainley make about how customers might view tattoos and body piercings?
6. Gainley argues that attitudes toward new trends will change with continued exposure to those trends. On what does she base this assumption? Could she have strengthened this part of the argument? How?

7. Does Gainley make concessions to the opposition? Where?
8. Trace the organization of the argument through each paragraph.
9. Are you persuaded by Gainley's argument? What parts are most convincing? Less convincing?
10. How does the tone of the essay contribute to the author's purpose?

Answers to Questions

1. "No organization should have to change to accommodate a candidate . . . as long as its standards are legal" (paragraph 10).
2. Premise 1: That we make assumptions about people based on appearances, which is the very argument the opposition claims is unfair. Premise 2: Employers must hire candidates that will not scare away customers. Therefore, the candidate for a job must change or choose a profession that accepts him or her as is.
3. The opposition is addressed in paragraphs 3, 4, 6, and 9. In 3, she addresses the maxim "You can't judge a book by its cover," which we can only assume was posited in the argument she is trying to refute (the high school editorial). In 4, she asserts that covers are intended to reveal, and in fact rely on people making assumptions. In 6, she addresses arguments that may have been made or could be made about freedom and discrimination and legality. In 9, she appeals to the opposition's belief in freedom.
4. In 9, she appeals to emotion and logic in the direct appeal to ideas of freedom and fairness. But she also appeals to reader's fear of not finding employment.
5. Gainley's first premise assumes that all people, which would include all customers, make assumptions based on appearances. Second, from this she assumes that because of this an unnamed number would take their business elsewhere. Third, she assumes that the number would be sufficient to negatively affect profits. Fourth, she assumes that profit outweighs expression. Students may find others.
6. She bases this assumption on one example—women wearing pants. She makes no distinctions between dress and permanent changes, such as tattoos. She could have strengthened this part of the argument by addressing that a tattoo, while a permanent adornment, is an enhancement made by choice. As such, it does not fall under the category of a "factor an applicant can't control." Students may have other opinions.
7. Her main concession comes in paragraph 1 when she states that "Every person has a need to be accepted," in paragraph 8 when she states we have the right to make personal choices, and in 9 when she states that those choices express whom we are.
8. The argument is traced thus: 1—Introduction orients reader to topic of job search and personal choice. 2—Addresses idea of acceptance, references back to high school and thus audience of job seekers, sets up a problem, and expands it to include body piercing and hairstyles. 3—Addresses the opposition's argument that "you can't judge a book by its cover" and attempts to refute it by asserting that covers are intended to reveal, and in fact rely on, people making assumptions. 4—Expands to include the idea that whole companies project an image, thereby likening companies to individuals, both of whom have choices. She uses this idea to segue into the idea of professional appearance. 5—Shifts the issue from freedom and fairness to the effects of appearance in the business world, thereby narrowing the topic and the discussion while dismissing the notion of fairness and providing a reason for judgment. 6—Addresses potential arguments about

freedom, discrimination, and legality; sets up a contrast and gives an example for support and comparison. In doing so, she returns to the idea of choice. 7—Provides personal testimony as evidence/support/authority on the subject of her basic premise that employers must hire those who will project their image so as to not scare away customers. 8—Argues that trends that continue will, over time, alter people's perceptions and that negative attitudes will shift to newer trends. This paragraph transitions back to the idea of consequences but now places the focus clearly on people that do not conform to expectations. 9—Restates the premises of the argument. 10—Concludes that the individual must change, not the organization.

9. Answers will vary.

10. The author's tone is for the most part reasonable. She sounds most disingenuous in paragraph 7 when she states that while she may not have "issues with visible tattoos or piercings," she cannot count on her customers not to have any biases.

C h a p t e r　30

Description

p. 633

■ **"A Day at the Theme Park" by W. Bruce Cameron—p. 633**

Questions on Content, Structure, and Style

1. What is Cameron's thesis and is it stated directly or implied?
2. What moods does Cameron convey in paragraph 2? What words or phrases contribute to these feelings?
3. What is the importance of the first sentence in paragraph 2?
4. Which of the five senses seems to predominate? What language indicates these versus others? Which other might have added to the general mood Cameron wished to inspire? How so? Give examples.
5. How do hyperbole and understatement contribute to Cameron's thesis?
6. Who is Cameron's audience? How can you tell?
7. Why does Cameron use the second-person pronoun "you" instead of the first-person pronoun "I" or a more objective third-person noun or pronoun?
8. What is the organizational strategy employed by Cameron?
9. How does the present tense contribute to Cameron's thesis?
10. How do the first and final paragraphs function to frame the essay and help establish a thesis?

Answers to Questions

1. Cameron's thesis is implied: children will take parents for a ride; letting them grow up may be difficult, revolting, frightening, but in the end they'll be glad to let go.

2. Answers will vary but here are a couple: "motion sickness and heat exhaustion"; "learn the boiling point of tennis shoes"—indicating pain and a feeling of being ill. As students explore this further they may see this paragraph as part of an extended metaphor for fear or dread or even hell.

3. The importance of the first sentence in paragraph 2 is that it provides the setting for this escapade, a contrast to the matter-of-fact tone found in paragraph 1, and a hint to the overall theme that toys with the notion of how things ought to be, rather than how they are. In the comparison of the theme park to an artificial vacation, Cameron poses a vacation that causes unanticipated stress, which is obviously antithetical to the nature of vacations. The additional sarcasm reveals that not only is the vacation not going to be pleasant, it will be downright painful. This sentence sets the reader up for the connection between parenting and stress.

4. Touch and sight seem to dominate in relation to the descriptions, but sound and smell could have further contributed to the mood: mixing diesel fumes with the pungent smells of a food court, or bloodcurdling screams, carousel music, and roller-coaster roars. However, one of these senses is far more selective—sound is possible to tune out—and the other could easily generate nostalgia, which is not the desired effect in this essay. Students will surely come up with their own ideas.

5. Hyperbole and understatement often work together to create a sense of imbalance, e.g., "though it seems a bit discourteous of them to have used pepper spray"—the juxtaposition of the polite attitude and the unexpected "pepper spray" mirror the sedateness found in maturity and the impetuosity of youth—the parent and the child.

6. Cameron's audience is obviously parents. He states it directly in paragraph 3: "The ride your children have selected for you . . ."

7. Cameron uses "you" to pull the reader along for the ride. Had he used first-person pronouns, the events would have been too personal and separate and he is writing to an idea more universal. Had he written using third person, the events would have not been as compelling because the internalized thoughts would have been more vicarious—a step further removed from reality-based experience.

8. Cameron's organizational strategy is to arrange a tour of the theme park as a way to reflect on relationships between parents and children, only in this case, the children are the unexpected guides—a bit of role reversal.

9. The present tense gives the essay immediacy and puts the reader in the park with the narrator and all of the feelings associated within, thereby allowing for a clearer perception of the disjointedness the narrator wants readers to feel.

10. The first and final paragraphs function to frame the essay and establish the author's theme of contrasts between expected roles and played roles, between expectations put on parents by society and children and the fears and confusions that role often puts parents in, between the desire to protect one's children and the desire to promote their growth.

Vocabulary

1. endearing (1)—being held in affection; being valued highly
2. fiendish (2)—a person displaying great wickedness; or the quality of intense pursuit, as in fanatical
3. discourteous (3)—not polite
4. acrophobia (5)—a fear of heights

■ "Hush Timmy—This Is Like a Church" by Kurt Andersen—p. 634

Questions on Content, Structure, and Style

1. What is the dominant impression Anderson intends his reader to have of the memorial? What metaphor does Anderson use to convey this impression?
2. What language choices help develop this metaphor?
3. A secondary theme is intertwined in the description, most notably in paragraphs 2, 5, and 10. What is this theme and what does it add to the description?
4. What kinds of research has Anderson done to create this very comprehensive description?
5. What are the most memorable details about the memorial? What do they add to the description?
6. In paragraph 2, Anderson gives his first visual description of the wall: "two skinny black granite triangles wedged onto a mound of Washington sod." What is the tone of that description? Why does he use such language and what is its effect?
7. Where does Anderson use elements of comparison and contrast to develop his description?
8. To what widely known quotation does the last line in paragraph 7 refer? How does this allusion develop the overall impression? How does the line relate to the physical wall itself?
9. Anderson quotes people with different connections to the memorial. What are those relationships? What does each add to the reader's understanding?
10. What place have you seen that has made an indelible impression on you? What metaphor might you use to enrich your description? What sorts of words and images could you use to emphasize the parallel? Whom could you interview to add depth and breadth to your personal perspective? What additional research would you need to do?

Answers to Questions

1. Anderson wants the reader to feel the memorial is a holy place at which the visitor has nearly a religious experience. Anderson uses a church as the unifying metaphor throughout.
2. Paragraph 1, "sanctum . . . spiritual place."
   Paragraph 6, "sublime and stirring."
   Paragraph 7, "hush, Timmy—This is like a church." (and, of course, the title)
   Paragraph 7, "processionals . . . ritual . . . liturgical . . . valley of the shadow of death."
   Paragraph 8, "a holy place."
   Paragraph 10, "faithful reflections."
3. Anderson also emphasizes the numerous unexpected contrasts and surprises connected to the wall. He sets up this motif in paragraph 2, "beautiful and terrible" and concludes this essay with a visitor's comment that "No one expected that [the eerie reflections of a plane reminiscent of Vietnam war planes]." The public's strong response was unexpected, Maya Lin's Asian connection is a strong irony, and the conflict over literal or symbolic

representations continues the tension of this theme. This secondary impression creates a feeling of ironic mystery and specialness to the memorial and underscores that the memorial has created a life of its own: "you don't set out and build a national shrine . . . It becomes one."

4. Interviews, historical information, visitor data, and details from the panels themselves are part of Anderson's research.

5. The number of names (58,022) help the reader relate to the enormity of the tragedy memorialized. Also, the increasingly large number of visitors shows that the mystique and power of the wall is growing rather than diminishing over time.

6. Anderson's tone is strikingly businesslike and purposely understates the impact of the memorial. His language emphasizes the simplicity of the concept and sets up a contrast to the complexity of its meaning and effect on the public.

7. In paragraph 3, the author compares the memorial to the other famous memorials to presidents in the capital. He also compares the two opposing views of what style the memorial should be. Later, in paragraph 7, he compares the wall to the Western Wall in Jerusalem, a Jewish religious shrine.

8. The line is taken from the Lord's Prayer. The allusion reminds the reader of the holiness of the church metaphor. After this line in the prayer comes "I shall fear no evil." The allusion enlarges the metaphoric meaning of the wall, a sanctuary, where visitors are protected, sheltered, and dramatically affected in the "valley" in the ground where the memorial is located.

9. The wall and statue's creators help clarify the purpose, history, and design of the memorial. The park ranger's words set the wall apart from other Washington memorials in its surprising impact; her comments come from much experience watching visitors at all the major monuments, so they have the ring of authority. The veterans' comments are poignant, relating the reader emotionally to the "wall experience," and validating the effectiveness and appropriateness of the memorial.

10. Students' responses will vary.

Vocabulary

1. redemptive (3)—serving to pay off or ransom
2. apolitical (4)—not relating to a particular political theory
3. elitist (5)—one who believes he or she is better than others by being part of a select or special group
4. stigmatized (5)—to mark or "brand" something as if it were disgraceful or not normal
5. sublime (6)—high in place; inspiring
6. figurative (6)—representative by likeness; typical
7. mandarins (6)—high, powerful officials
8. spectral (6)—resembling a ghost or spirit
9. wary (6)—cautious, suspicious
10. erstwhile (7)—at one time; former
11. liturgical (7)—having to do with prayer or worship
12. touchstone (7)—a test for genuineness
13. catharsis (7)—a purifying change
14. amphitheatrical (7)—like a valley or level place surrounded by rising ground similar to an ancient theater with seats rising up the circular sides
15. totem (8)—an animal or object taken to be a symbol of a clan

■ "The Way to Rainy Mountain" by N. Scott Momaday—p. 636

Questions on Content, Structure, and Style

1. Momaday's narrator is clearly reminiscing, but of what?

2. Momaday seamlessly blends time, shifting from era to era as though it is all one memory. What does this technique add to your understanding of the journey taking place?

3. What does Momaday mean in paragraph one by "the prairie is an anvil's edge" and how does this knowledge fit into his theme of rebirth?

4. Momaday's use of figurative language permeates his descriptions. Discuss the effects of the following: "the steaming foliage seems almost to writhe in fire" (1), "they entered the world through a hollow log" (4), "they were bent and blind in the wilderness" (6), ". . . clouds that sail . . . are shadows that move upon the grain like water, dividing light" (7).

5. Where do you find some examples of personification and how do they contribute to the piece?

6. "Here and there on dark stones were ancestral names (15). What other lines in the story are echoed here?

7. What is the function of paragraph 11?

8. The narrator retells the "legend at the base of the rock"—Devil's Tower—in paragraph eight. He then states that "so long as the legend lives the Kiowas have kinsmen in the night sky." To what exactly is he referring and how does it work into the frame story?

9. In paragraph 14, Momaday juxtaposes the smallness of his grandmother's house and the giant size of the cricket that "filled the moon like a fossil." To what is he referring in the line that follows: "It had gone there, I thought, to live and die, for there of all places, was its small definition made whole and eternal."

10. In the final paragraph the author writes, "Looking back once, I saw the mountain and came away. Why is this visit to the grave so brief?

Answers to Questions

1. The narrator is reminiscing of the following: his grandmother—p. 3, 4, 5, 9, 10; his people—p.3, 4, 6, 7, 8, 9, 12, 13; the land of his ancestors—p. 2, 7, 8, 15; his own travels—p.6, 7, 8; his childhood—p. 10, 12, 13; and his grandmother's house—p. 1 and 14. In paragraph 11 he is not reminiscing.

2. Responses will vary but some discussion should ensue about its being more than a physical journey to visit a grave. This is a spiritual ancestral memory brought to light in writing. It pays tribute to the author's people, acknowledging grief and suffering as equal challenges to spirit and survival. His grandmother's death provides the impetus for the journey, which then becomes the vehicle for transforming grief and comprehending its role in the larger journey of life. There is a theme of rebirth into new understanding and giving new life to the past by conveying stories from the past.

3. In this metaphor the prairie is likened to an anvil's edge. The anvil, used to shape iron in the presence of fire, represents the unyielding heat of the prairie at Rainy Mountain where the "hardest weather in the world is" (4). Momaday comes back to this idea repeatedly, suggesting that those who can survive it are strong.

4. Responses will vary. Having students deal with explaining how they are affected will help them connect more closely to the text and come to comprehend Momaday's connection to earth more clearly. Not all students will have experiential knowledge of the rural and wild earth that Momaday reveals and, therefore, a general discussion on this question may help broaden horizons, so to speak.

5. Personification is abundant in paragraph seven: "Sweet clover takes hold of the hills," "the sun is at home on the plains," the oldest deity (Sol) ranging after the solstices," and one not quite as easy to see involves the "northern winter" as a mother figure when her progeny move south and must "wean" themselves from her climate.

6. These words take us directly back to paragraph 11: "They stand *here* and *there* against the sky . . . ." References to his ancestors are clear in the final paragraph, but now we can clarify the meaning of the sentinel houses in paragraph 11.

7. Paragraph 11 functions to shift the story from his ancestor's memories to his own childhood memories by using the houses on the plains as a metaphor for his ancestors. When he states that "you approach them for a longer time than you expect," he entreats the reader to participate in his movement through time, asking us, if you will, to see life and death as universal experiences but also shifting us to his own memories.

8. He refers directly to the Big Dipper, which is associated with the North Star and navigation. From this we understand that his ancestors discovered how to leave the northern mountains and travel south. Devil's Tower probably functioned as a compass, of sorts. Moreover, with "kinsmen in the night sky" the Kiowas acknowledged themselves as part of the universe they traversed, and it of them. In this way, the telling of the legend passes along a belief system to succeeding generations. The retelling here functions to explain that "story" is strong in passing along traditions, but it also teaches that if one follows the path of tradition, one can find one's way out of darkness. This idea is key to the frame story of a pilgrimage begun in grief and ended in acceptance.

9. The "It" in this sentence would seem to refer to the cricket and may do so on one level of understanding in which he imagines the cricket as part of the universe that extends beyond mortality. But we might also read this passage to refer to "His line of vision," for then we can connect his sense of "seeing with the mind's eye" (5) what his grandmother had known about Rainy Mountain and what he eventually left with—an understanding of his own place in the chain of ancestors and the universe itself.

10. The journey's destination was not the place but the alteration of spirit and mind. He had attained that the night before. Physical completion of the trek ended at the grave, but the grave itself had no more compulsion than the houses on the plain, for death is not something one seeks and understanding of it is best left to time.

Vocabulary

1. anvil (1)—a large piece of iron used by blacksmiths to forge iron into various shapes
2. writhe (1)—to wriggle and sway
3. preeminently (3)—first and foremost
4. disposition (3)—a person's tendency toward a particular type of behavior
5. stores (3)—provisions—food and other items that sustain life
6. awful (8)—full of awe, reverence, or amazement
7. tenuous (8)—sketchy, not certain
8. deicide (9)—the erasure (murder) of a deity or god in the minds or actions of a people
9. ample (12)—plentiful or large
10. enmities (12)—feelings of ill will toward another
11. mourning (14)—a period of grief or sadness for the loss of a loved one
12. scissortail (15)—bird, specifically a flycatcher, with a deeply forked tail
13. hied (15)—fled quickly

Chapter 31

Narration

p. 641

- ■ **"38 Who Saw Murder Didn't Call the Police"**
  by Martin Gansberg—p. 641

Questions on Content, Structure, and Style

1. Does Gansberg's article have a thesis? What is it?
2. What point of view does Gansberg use? Who tells the story? What advantages and/or limitations does his narrative choice present?
3. In some ways Gansberg's article is a factual newspaper account of the Genovese incident; in other ways it seems more like fiction. Explain his technique.
4. Evaluate Gansberg's tone in this essay. What seems to be his attitude toward his subject?
5. Note the modifiers—especially the adverbs—that Gansberg uses when he records the statements of the witnesses. What does his choice of words reveal about these people?
6. What, apparently, were Gansberg's main sources for the facts of the Genovese case?
7. How does Gansberg structure his essay? What organizational pattern does he employ?
8. Why does Gansberg include the two paragraphs about the arrest of the suspect? Is the information given here necessary to the point he's trying to make? Does it add to the story?
9. What effect does the material presented in paragraphs 11–16 have? How can Gansberg know these details? Is this a good tactic for writers of descriptive essays?
10. What reason might Gansberg have for including the information about the cost of the homes in the neighborhood where the incident occurred? Is this relevant? Why or why not?

Answers to Questions

1. Whether the article has a thesis in the usual sense of the word is debatable, but it certainly presents a point of view. The implied "thesis" is that the United States is a nation of individuals so fearful of "getting involved" that they will stand by and watch while their fellow beings are murdered.

2. He uses a third-person, omniscient narrator. The author is absent from the piece; the nameless narrator is able to recount events that could realistically not be known by the author, except secondhand. However, he tells the story as though he were always present.

3. In part, Gansberg's piece is similar to the contemporary style of blending fact and fiction that some have called "faction." The story is based on fact, but Gansberg, rather than simply recording the facts, creates a short-story effect by the way he uses a narrator, records dialogue, etc.

4. Although the narrative "voice" offers no direct comment, it is clear from what is said that Gansberg is horrified by what happened and finds the incident symptomatic of a major social problem. He obviously feels compassion for Genovese and disdain for those who failed to help her.

5. He has people say things "sheepishly," "knowingly if quite casually," "without emotion." They shrug, peek out from behind partly closed doors—in short, they seem every bit as uncaring and aloof as one might expect from the facts.

6. The police and Genovese's neighbors. Most likely, his story is based, at least in part, on earlier news accounts.

7. He begins in the present, then recounts the Genovese murder in chronological order, then he introduces the fact of the suspect's arrest and closes with the witnesses' comments.

8. From the standpoint of the Genovese story and the point Gansberg is making about what happened, the material is probably unnecessary. However, from a journalistic standpoint, the material is significant and it probably answers (as well as could be expected at the time) questions most readers would ask.

9. The details could have come in part from the witnesses' accounts, but much of it is certainly fictional—Gansberg's way of dramatizing the incident and stressing the horror the victim felt. One appalling side note that instructors might point out regarding this horror felt by Genovese and other victims: in 1995 Genovese's murderer, Winston Mosely, stated to parole officials that he has suffered more than his victim because for her it was "a one-minute affair, but for the person who's caught, it's forever."

10. The facts and figures indicate that the neighborhood is upper-middle to middle-class (remember this is 1964) and composed primarily of single-family dwellings. Though Gansberg does not say so, the implication is clear: if it can happen here it can happen anywhere. These are presumably well-to-do, hard-working, successful people. Yet they failed to respond the way we might expect they should.

Vocabulary

1. recitation (4)—account, as if by rote
2. staid (6)—reserved, grave
3. distraught (26)—upset, worried

■ "Crossing the Great Divide" by Peter Fish—p. 644

Questions on Content, Structure, and Style

1. Who is the audience for this essay?
2. What is the importance of Fish visiting South Pass before visiting it with his wife and son?
3. Why does Fish want his four-month-old son to see something he is unlikely to remember?
4. How does the Continental Divide operate as the dominant image in this essay?
5. Identify the major organizational pattern.
6. What other patterns are present? Where?
7. What does the writer mean by "At South Pass it's just you and the weight of hopes so numerous they dent the earth a century and a half later"?
8. What is the effect of including Cecelia Adams's diary entry in paragraph 6: "It ill comports with the ideas we have formed of a pass through the Rocky Mountains, being merely a vast, level and sandy plain sloping a little on each side of the summit"?
9. What does a "short growing season" have to do with wagon ruts still existing? Why are the ruts important?
10. Compare the ideas surrounding wagon ruts to the ideas found in paragraph 5: ". . . though a national historic landmark, it is noticeably lacking in the visitor centers, interpretive trails, and gift shops with which Americans embalm their history."

Answers to Questions

1. Both the public with a penchant for travel logs and the writer's son.
2. Fish needs to visit in order to gather the historical information he will include in his travel log, which will serve as a history for his son in later years. It is possible, of course, that the writer did not actually make a separate trip and that this is a rhetorical device intended to allow the reader to see and listen as he did, without the additional filters of his wife and son. In effect, he can write his thoughts on his own perceptions and reactions rather than those of his family.
3. To "commemorate passing time," but here the act is symbolic—a birthday celebration via the remembrance of others. As a birthday celebration, it is the gift of ideas he wants his son to appreciate and they are recorded in his own hand, thereby giving his son a legacy of thought and self.
4. The Continental Divide represents both the variety of divisions perceived in life—past and present, east and west, old and new, youth and age, height and depth, life and death. As an image, it looms large as a place in a vast mountain chain, hard sought and found. It represents the hope the emigrants had when they crossed it, but also the struggles they had in finding their way to and over it. South Pass resides there and stands in stark contrast to perceptions of grandeur that the Rockies represent.
5. The major organizational pattern should be readily apparent as chronological narrative.
6. Other patterns involve a secondary major focus on comparison and contrast and description of place. Examples will vary, but a few include the age of the author vs. his son; "look forward and backward, like a driver shifting his gaze from the windshield to the rearview mirror"; the modernity of a "government truck" driving on "highway 28" vs. the history of South Pass; the Divide itself, where you can "splash your canteen and half

the water would go to the Atlantic and half to the Pacific"; the response to South Pass that travelers have had, such as shooting "rifles in the air and" shouting "Huzzah!'" while "others turned introspective." Descriptions of place come with the carved names in "splintered granite," rising "with Wyoming toward the sky," "At the end of dirt road was a stone slab inscribed . . ." and "He was dressed as a 19th century sharpie in wool pants and a vest that resembled mattress ticking." Students will surely find other examples.

7. Interpretations will vary, but it is important that students see the juxtaposition of ruts and hopes—that the hope for a better life caused people to carve the earth for their use and yet left only those wagon ruts behind, only harmless dents, yet dents that speak to generations afterward about human dreams and pursuits.

8. Again, answers will vary, but a few key elements need discussion: the fact that South Pass is not impressive, yet it represents a far larger imagined space, a freer space, if you will. As a metaphor for hope, it is a spiritual and emotional renewal, or change, or progress toward something not always definitive, but rather known as better than whatever place one is in, or has been in, that has not been quite as satisfying as expected. While the emigrant moves physically from one place to another, place comes to represent both the desire itself and the movement toward it. We call this living. The thoughtful student will recognize that place isn't always concrete/tactile. This might be a good time to discuss the use of concrete imagery to express abstract ideas.

9. The "short growing season" for city dwellers may not mean a great deal. Students will certainly have some references about seasons and geography but may not grasp the finer details: a short season of spring indicates long winters and early summers—both seasons can be perceived as dry. Even though snow indicates moisture, the cold temperatures counter the retention of moisture as a required nutrient for growth, in the immediate sense. Thus, not much can grow over the ruts and neither can much wash them away. Therefore, the ruts are preserved. One might think that modern society might have paved them over, but they have been preserved in a different manner by that same society. So while nature preserves history by not "embalming" the ruts with seed or effluence, it does so through the absence of such, thus teaching a lesson in balance as well as offering humanity an opportunity to participate in its own growth. This essay is as much about conservation as it is about legacy and hope. It should be noted that the essay was published in *Sunset* magazine, a periodical devoted to preservation and appreciation of the Western United States.

10. When we compare the idea of short growing seasons to historic landmarks that have not been "embalmed," we can view South Pass as having survived, like the ruts, despite a lack of seed or effluence/glitz or glam/spice or billboards the like of which advertise the place itself, rather than what it might represent as a monument to human faith and hope.

Vocabulary

1. commemorate (1)—to remember through observance or celebration
2. sharpie (5)—a well-dressed man, often thought to be a con man
3. spiking (5)—embellishing; adding to make more appealing
4. embalm (5)—to protect from decay or to preserve by filling up with spices or sterilizing fluid
5. comports (6)—agrees, behaves (in relation to one's demeanor)
6. disparaged (9)—spoke about in an unkind manner
7. unflappable (13)—calm, serene

■ "The Talkies" by James Lileks—p. 646

Questions on Content, Structure, and Style

1. The first paragraph of this essay tells the reader what the writer is not going to write about. Why does Lileks begin this way?
2. Throughout the essay, Lileks uses dialogue—he repeats the words of the movie talkers. What does this add to the essay?
3. When does Lileks announce his distinct purpose in writing this essay?
4. What specific names and places does Lileks use to add reality to this essay?
5. To what senses of the reader does Lileks appeal as he retells his experience?
6. How does Lileks attempt to be fair in his condemnation of the talkers?
7. While entertainment is probably not the main purpose of this essay, Lileks maintains a humorous tone throughout. Why does he adopt this approach?
8. Which detail was most memorable and why?
9. This essay comes from *Notes of a Nervous Man*. What other public annoyances do you suppose make Lileks "nervous"?
10. What is a pet peeve of yours? Describe one specific time you encountered it.

Answers to Questions

1. Lileks uses these universal experiences so that the audience will identify with the movie-going experience and irritations generally associated with it. He is setting a tone of annoyance that the audience can identify with.
2. Repeating the exact dialogue of the talkers adds a sense of reality and helps the reader picture the incident more clearly.
3. In paragraph 23, Lileks tells moviegoers to think before they talk long and continually through a movie, spoiling the experience for the rest of the audience.
4. Using names such as Siskel and Ebert, Dots, Curious George, Gene Hackman, and Willem Dafoe validates the narrative and the reader can experience its details with the writer.
5. In paragraph 1, Lileks appeals to sight, sound, touch, and taste. The rest of the details are primarily sight and sound.
6. Lileks tries to be reasonable by stating, in paragraph 3, that he can understand a whispered or limited comment; it is the loud and persistent comments that he is protesting.
7. The humorous tone may take enough edge off his anger that readers can identify themselves in the essay and respond positively. Also, readers who are not the talkers can enjoy the essay more and can laugh along with Lileks since they have probably had similar experiences.
8. Student responses will vary; however, most can point to a specific detail that stuck in their minds.
9. Although there are many other public annoyances that probably would bother Lileks, students might pick up on paragraph 17, where Lileks indicates he is a smoker and his behavior might bother others as much as talkers bother him!
10. Students will have different pet peeves to discuss.

Vocabulary

1. decibels (3)—units for measuring sound
2. empirical (5)—based on numerous experiences
3. epiphany (5)—a moment of sudden understanding
4. malicious (7)—with mean intentions
5. nostalgic (7)—causing a longing for something long ago
6. telekinesis (18)—the movement of an object caused while not in contact with the body generating the force: "mind over matter"
7. sodium pentothal (21)—a truth drug
8. mole (21)—a dark-colored, raised spot or mark on the skin

Chapter 32

Essays for Further Analysis: Multiple Strategies and Styles

p. 649

■ **"I Have a Dream" by Martin Luther King, Jr.—p. 649**

Questions on Content, Structure, and Style

1. King's "I Have a Dream" is a speech rather than an essay. What stylistic tactics does he use that seem especially effective for oral presentation?
2. Considering King's audience, what might be the main purpose of his speech? Is his intent to be persuasive?
3. Analyze King's opening sentence. Why is it appropriate?
4. What extended analogy does King use when discussing the Constitution and the Declaration of Independence? Is the metaphor a good one?
5. One rhetorical tactic that King employs especially well is repetition. Give examples of his use of this device.
6. What is the effect of repetition generally? In King's speech?
7. King is noted for his belief in both racial harmony and nonviolent protest. Does this speech reflect that belief?

8. King quotes from both the Declaration of Independence and the song "America." What effect does this have on his message?
9. What word (and its variants) is used most often in this speech? Why is it important?
10. Is King's argument logical or emotional? Does he appeal to our minds or our hearts?

Answers to Questions

1. The most obvious device is repetition. It should be noted as well that his language is rhythmical and simple, and his sentences short—terse and emphatic.
2. King's primary audience shared his beliefs. In this sense, the speech may be seen more as an inspirational message than persuasive discourse.
3. The "Five score years ago" echoes the beginning of Lincoln's Emancipation Proclamation. The "great American" is Lincoln, and King is standing in the shadow of the Lincoln Memorial. The speech was given at a massive protest march celebrating the Emancipation Proclamation.
4. He compares the two documents to a check. His analogy is both appropriate and consistent.
5. See paragraphs 2, 4, 11–18, 20–27.
6. Repetition is used for emphasis. In speeches it works especially well because of the limitations placed on the audience. Readers are able to follow points much more easily, for example, and can reread if necessary. King, in this speech, frequently uses extended passages in which he employs repetition—for example, the repeated phrase "I have a dream." This not only underscores his point, but also contrasts with the reality he describes.
7. Yes. See paragraphs 6 and 7.
8. The quotes, which reflect the American ideal, offer a contrast to the American reality. King's dream is only to have that reality fulfilled. By citing lines that Americans know well and believe in, he emphasizes the point that blacks only want the rights held dear by all Americans.
9. The word is "free" (or the variant "freedom"). Freedom, of course, is the subject both of the speech and of King's "dream." Again, this speech was delivered at a celebration of the Emancipation Proclamation, which freed slaves in America.
10. Though the ideas presented are grounded in logic, the overall tone of the speech is emotional.

Vocabulary

1. languishing (2)—without energy or spirit, weak
2. inextricably (6)—tangled, too complex to unravel

■ "Beauty: When the Other Dancer Is the Self" by Alice Walker—p. 652

Questions on Content, Structure, and Style

1. What is the significance of Walker's title? What does it mean?
2. What point of view does Walker use in this essay? Who is the narrator?
3. What verb tense is this essay written in? Where, in time, does the author "stand" in relation to the events she is describing? How does this relate to her method of organization?

4. In several instances Walker uses italics. Why? How do these passages differ from the others?

5. Why, in the first few episodes she recounts, does Walker place so much emphasis on clothing—what she wore, what people thought of her garments, etc.?

6. How does the scar change the narrator? How does this relate to the thesis, or main point, of the essay?

7. Why does Walker include the poem "On Sight" in her essay? How does it contribute to the meaning of her essay?

8. What does Walker's daughter see in the blind eye? How does this change the author's perception of her scar? herself?

9. Evaluate the final paragraph. Is this an effective conclusion? Why or why not?

10. This is obviously a personal essay, one that records a specific problem in the life of one individual. Is it more than that? Does the general theme of Walker's essay have universal application?

Answers to Questions

1. The title refers to her metaphorical quest—in the essay—for the meaning of beauty. It also refers to the incident (and the idea) related in the final paragraph. She has come to terms with her past, her other self.

2. She uses the first person. Obviously, she is writing a personal experience essay, but it might be pointed out to students that a first-person narrative does not always mean that the author and the narrator are the same person.

3. She is reflecting on past events, but she uses the present tense. This underscores the reflective nature of the essay. Notice that she uses age as a focal point for each episode and that the organization is chronological.

4. The italic passages represent the voice of the narrator in the present. Because past episodes are related in present tense as well, the italics serve to distinguish between past and present, between the old and new "self." Too, they function as transitional devices.

5. This stresses the difference between superficial, or external, beauty and the deeper beauty she comes to discover within herself.

6. The scar changes the nature of the girl completely—or, at least, she thinks so. She has not fundamentally changed, but because she has been so aware of external beauty—her clothes, her appearance, her action—she feels who she is has been radically altered. The wound makes her "blind" in more ways than one.

7. This passage is pivotal to the essay. Suddenly recalling—and confronting—the words of the doctor about the possibility of losing sight in both eyes, Walker learns, for the first time, to really see. The desert is bleak, not of interest to most people, who would say it is all the same, monotonous. Walker learns that the desert has beauty. She looks past the "flags" of vision—the symbols—and really sees. This passage provides transition from one state and time to another.

8. The child sees an image that resembles the picture of the earth taken from the moon that appears on *Big Blue Marble*. Walker has to this point been uneasy about her daughter looking at the scarred eye. When she asks, "Mommy, where did you get that world in your eye?" the pain—most of it anyway—leaves.

9. The conclusion is highly effective. It relates to the title (see question 1 above) and brings the essay full circle. The final episode is a resolution of the conflict within herself that the author recounts.

10. The essay has universal application, as most effective personal experience essays do. Readers will not have the same specific problem, but they may have some problem that creates self-doubt and dissatisfaction.

Vocabulary

1. crinolines (4)—billowing underskirts made from a stiff, starched fabric
2. boisterous (16)—rowdy

■ "A Modest Proposal" by Jonathan Swift—p. 657

Questions on Content, Structure, and Style

1. What are the narrator's main reasons for boiling babies? To what does he appeal?
2. Where is the narrator's proposal first stated? Is this his thesis?
3. Who is the audience for this essay?
4. Identify some terms used for the people whose children will be eaten. What effect might they have on the intended reader?
5. In paragraph 18 Swift mentions a man by the name of Psalmanazar, a Frenchman who falsely identified himself as a Formosan and who wrote a fictional account of Formosa as a land of cannibals. This fellow was accepted, initially, into the homes of the upper classes as a "fellow to know." That he was an impostor tells us something about the gullibility of humans. What does it say about Swift's intent?
6. Recalling that a narrator should be differentiated from the author, consider what Swift's purpose is in having his narrator propose that Irish children of a certain age be eaten for the greater good.
7. Is there logic in the structure of this essay? Explain.
8. What metaphor do you find in paragraph 12? What is its purpose?
9. Is this essay humorous? If so, in what way(s)? If not, why not?
10. Can you think of any political satirists living today? How might they compare with Swift?

Answers to Questions

1. The narrator claims to want to alleviate poverty (1), the "prodigious number of children" (2), and abortions (5) while providing a service by contributing to the "feeding, and partly to the clothing, of many thousands (4). The appeals here are not to one's sense of justice, but to one's annoyance caused by the poor with many children. Meanwhile, paragraphs 21–28 list the "advantages" of the scheme and thus also provide reasons for enacting his proposal. The appeals in the latter are aimed at the audience's greed.
2. Paragraph nine issues the proposal even though he never directly states that he wants to sell babies as food. He instead refers to being advised that a "child well nursed is at a year old a most delicious, nourishing, and wholesome food . . ." (9). This would seem to be the narrator's thesis, but not Swift's.
3. The piece is clearly focused to landlords, as evidenced by the barb in paragraph 12, but the narrator also refers to "our city of Dublin" and so appeals to all living there or representing it.
4. We find "beggars" and "thieves" (1), "dam" (4), "women murdering their bastard children" (5), "savages" (10), "Papists" (13). All but the last should paint these parents in a

distinctly negative light for today's audience. The intended audience of Swift's era would comprehend the final adjective to be equally offensive, as there had long been a rift between the Anglican and the Catholic churches. The effect, however, might be one of subtle disapproval, and perhaps violent disapproval. Students responses will vary.

5. That Swift uses this character as a responsible source of information allows the knowledgeable reader to wink at the satire and the jab to heads of state who feast on the demise of their own citizenry for their own pleasures.

6. Clearly, Swift himself cannot and would not propose such a ludicrous and immoral idea as serious. Not only would it denigrate his position in the church, it would reveal him a fool and an equal to the landlords with whom he's taken issue. But it might also put him in the precarious position of having to defend himself against charges of proposing mass murder. Putting the piece into the hands of a fictional narrator allows him to shame his intended audience while claiming it is just fiction.

7. As an argument, Swift takes a position by positing a problem and providing a solution that, but for its basic immorality, functions to resolve a great many issues having to do with poverty. Unfortunately, he has a good many fallacies—citing faulty authorities, attacking the character of the poor, appeals to emotional reactions, diversionary tactics, and assuming that the poverty of the Irish was directly caused by the number of children they had.

8. Swift compares landlords to animals devouring prey or cannibals in the way they strip tenants of their ability to survive financially. The metaphor serves to squarely place blame for the impoverishment of the Irish. It also counters his fallacious argument that the poor have created their own position and thus he places blame where he believes it rightly belongs.

9. Responses will vary.

10. Responses will vary. Some to note might include the likes of political comedians Jon Stewart and Bill Maher, or cartoonists such as MacGruder of *Boondocks* and Trudeau of *Doonesbury*.

Vocabulary

■ Note: Some of Swift's terms carried somewhat different meanings in his day than they would for us today.

1. *modest (title)—inexpensive (rather than demure or chaste)
2. fricassee (9)—a stew, generally of a light colored meat in a light or brown gravy
3. ragout (9)—meat and vegetables in a thick sauce
4. *projectors (4)—schemers, those who put forth ideas
5. *parts (6)—promising abilities, talents
6. *dear (12)—expensive (in addition to cherished or kind)
7. repine (14)—complain or express dejection
8. *artificially (15)—skillfully
9. *shambles (16)—slaughterhouses
10. *distress (22)—from distraint: seizing property by legal means in order to pay debts

Chapter  33
Literature
p. 665

■ **"Perhaps the World Ends Here" by Joy Harjo—p. 665**

Questions on Content, Structure, and Style

1. List the lines you read literally. List those read figuratively. Where can you read both ways?
2. Discuss the imagery in line 13. What does it conjure up in your imagination?
3. What images are conjured in lines 2 and 3? What do they add to the feeling of the poem?
4. Lines 10–12 seem the most enigmatic. What does Harjo mean by "Our dreams drink coffee with us as they put their arms around our children"?
5. Why do you think lines 10–12 are in the middle of the poem?
6. Do lines 14 and15 suggest a place outside the family or not? Explain.
7. In the margin of your text, draw lines horizontally to represent lines in the poem that you think are literal and vertical lines to represent those that are figurative (next to the lines themselves). What do your drawings suggest to you about the poem's structure?
8. There is no rhyme scheme, per se, in this poem, but there is alliteration, iteration, and assonance. What do you note about its use in lines14–19?
9. What does the kitchen table in this poem represent?
10. What does Harjo mean in lines 20 and 21? How do these lines complete the poem?

Answers to Questions

1. Lines that can be read literally are the second part of line 1 and again at line 3; the first part of line 4; lines 5, 7, 9, and the second sentence of line 14 and 15; 18 and 19. Lines that can be read figuratively include the first part of line 1, the second part of 4; line 8, 10, 11, 12, the first part of 14; and lines 20 and 21. Lines 13, 16 and 17 can be read both ways. Individual readers may argue that all of the lines are figurative, or literal, or both. It is important to note that the author's meaning relies on some of them being read literally because our life experience is often literal and that we give it extended meaning by choice.

2. Responses will vary, but most readers will see the table as house and table as umbrella as a child would use a table outdoors—a type of fort, a protective device. But in this understanding we shouldn't neglect the additional component that is less literal—the table as family. Students may view the table in the figurative differently. Exploring ways to see it is useful to understanding the theme.

3. These two lines suggest a relation of table to altar. The phrasing echoes that found in the Bible and while this line can be read initially as literal, the final sentences allude to something more reverent. The reverential feeling gives the poem depth and asks the reader to look more closely.

4. Responses will again vary. What dreams represent is anyone's guess. On the one hand they could be read literally as dreams and thus the arrangement becomes the poetry, so that we drink coffee while our dreams entertain us (our imagination). We imagine our children—which we'll have, perhaps. The table becomes a place to laugh at our errors— to share them and to recover from them and to grow with the help of others, including our kids. Or perhaps the kids are our errors and from them we learn.

5. However these lines make sense to a reader, they should be understood in the context of the entire structure. Falling in the center gives them importance when we look at the topic of the poem as a table. What is the centerpiece? Because these lines are more enigmatic than others, the notion of centerpiece is stressed and we are forced to examine the lines more closely in the context of a frame. Here the table is less important than the images situated around it. Thus *family* love and life becomes the dominant theme. Many of the other images echo this idea.

6. Here "wars" can be read as those that are fought at the kitchen table, because that is the table Harjo first defines. But we can extend the metaphor if we choose and these are the lines that allow us to do so. Here we can expand our notion of family to include all of humanity as sharing in one table.

7. This is a visual experiment designed to bring the reader closer to the frame of the poem. Vertical and horizontal lines might represent the parts of the poem as in parts of a table—planks, legs—and in lines 10–12, even a circle or table top. The whole suggests parts and the puzzle is in putting the parts together. Harjo's theme of life is puzzle-like in that where we expect a poem not to be literal, much of hers is. This upsets expectations, forcing us to re-see the obvious—the literal—and experience the kitchen table as more than a piece of furniture. Other interpretations along these lines will help further understanding.

8. In these lines, sound functions to compare and contrast ideas: "birth" borrows in "burial"; "terror" and "terrible" juxtapose "shadow" and "place to celebrate"; "sing" befriends "sorrow," " suffering," "remorse," and "thanks." The jumble of contrasts is both dissonant

and compelling in the way jazz is. This underlying impression of musical sound lends some conversation to the table—the murmur, if you will, of the emotions that might be found in the events described.

9. By now it should be readily apparent the table is life.

10. Lines 20 and 21 complete the poem by completing the idea of life. Here the world represents the physical and thus when we die, the physical world comes to an end.

■ "Ozymandias" by Percy Bysshe Shelley—p. 666

Questions on Content, Structure, and Style

1. Who or what is Ozymandias?
2. Who is the speaker in the poem and does his or her role contribute to the poem's meaning?
3. What primary images are presented and what might they represent?
4. What is the dominant impression?
5. What words suggest allusions and to what?
6. The author of your textbook notes that this poem is a sonnet. What does the sonnet structure lend to the meaning of the poem?
7. Where in the poem is the imagery most difficult to follow? Why?
8. What does Shelley reveal as the one thing that survives in this scenario? How is this relevant to the overall meaning?
9. What is the mood of the piece?
10. The Romantic poets offered a variety of styles and subjects for reflection. They also broke with convention in order to reveal connections with and among everyday people. To do so, they often juxtaposed the exotic and the common. Here Shelley explores both. What does such an effort provide the reader with in this poem?

Answers to Questions

1. Students will note that the poem states he was a king and may be able to determine that a statue was erected to him, but if they have read the footnote they will also note he was the Egyptian king Ramses II and that he built the statue of himself. They will also note that his name comes from the Greek.

2. The speaker of the poem is unidentified but is important to the meaning as he or she is relating a tale told by another of sights from an ancient land. The power of the word is important here, the passing along of lost or potentially lost information, the history of time and place that the traveler wishes to convey.

3. The concrete images are only the broken pieces of statue and the desert sands. While answers will vary, here are some focused possibilities that need recognition: the statue represents civilization through the literal representation of a man and a king (order, art, etc.); the size of the statue represents great wealth and power—a tribute to the man and the civilization he represents; the statue's decomposition represents the decay, corruption, loss, destruction or fall of the man himself and/or the civilization he represents; the desert represents decomposition itself, a natural tomb of sorts, and the idea of time passing, of loss through natural processes, etc.

4. The idea of an arid environment that cannot sustain physical life or even monuments to it may more fully describe the dominant impression.

5. Students may not see any allusions, so some may need explanation, as in "king of kings," which has a general biblical reference and specifically relates to Jesus of Nazareth/Christ. Once this allusion is understood, the inscription on the statue's base can be evaluated more fully. Another allusion is the inscription itself, which is a direct reference to the one found on the original Colossus in Egypt, according to the Greek historian Diodorus Siculus. It read, "I am Ozymandias, king of kings; if anyone wishes to know what I am and where I lie, let him surpass me in some of my exploits."

6. Answers will vary, but a few options include the fact that several lines do not follow the predictable pattern of rhyme found in the Spenserian sonnet, which is the closest rhyme scheme suggested by the pattern that does exist. The ababa pattern is an aberration. The couplet cannot be formed in any way.

   Therefore, the final couplet has been forced out by the aberrant line 5. It could be argued that line 4 is the aberrant line as it contains a rhyme of consonance only (with the final "n" sound), but if one does not treat this as a rhyme of consonance then both lines fall into question and command the reader's attention. What would have been a continuing rhyme is aborted and then resumed, much like the power of Ozymandias and his legend—broken and taken up again in the poem itself.

7. Line 8 is particularly ambiguous as it leaves the reader attempting to "re-attach" the concrete images of a hand and a heart to the statue. This line is often read, though, as the sculptor's hand and the king's heart—both now lifeless but once full of passion. Lines 4 and 5 feed this idea.

8. Passion.

9. Melancholy or hope, depending on one's point of view. Answers will vary.

10. Answers will vary here as well and can provide an opportunity for a writing assignment that employs poetic explication.

■ "Dulce Et Decorum Est" by Wilfred Owen—p. 667

Questions on Content, Structure, and Style

1. Describe the setting and mood in this poem.
2. Who is the speaker in Owen's poem? What line(s) in the poem indicate this?
3. Trace the tone of voice in this poem. How does it change from stanza to stanza?
4. What is the rhyme scheme here?
5. Why are lines 15 and 16 separated from those above and below them? How do they function to unify or highlight ideas in the poem?
6. Owen's imagery is at times quite graphic. To what is he referring in lines 11–14?
7. In line six, Owen notes that the men "All went lame; all blind." Do you think he's being literal here? What effect is he working toward in this stanza?
8. What does line 20 suggest about the soldier's expression?
9. The horrors of war in this poem are relived in the dreams that haunt the survivors— lines 15–16. What is Owen's message to the reader?
10. This poem does not fit into traditional ideologies of war and patriotism. What response do you have to it in this sense?

Answers to Questions

1. The setting is somewhere in Europe during WWI, but it could be any war in which soldiers were or are asked to march or move through hostile terrain, laden with heavy packs and artillery. The mood is bleak and dark.

2. The speaker is an infantryman reliving horrifying moments of being gassed by the Five-Nines exploding behind them.

3. The tone moves from weariness to frantic fear and confusion to horror and hateful pain and then to accusation and bitter warning.

4. The rhyme scheme is quite regular in its repetition of *abab cdcd efef* until line 14 where Owen repeats *e*, so that it reads *gege*, thus folding the stanza back onto itself. He again picks up a regular rhyme at line 17 to complete the poem.

5. The speaker in lines 1–14 does not speak directly to the audience, so that there seems to be more narrative memory functioning here. Whereas in lines 17–28 there is direct address and admonishment—an attempt to frighten the reader with images and invitation to see what he saw during war, not merely relate a tale of war. In lines 15 and 16 the speaker is dreaming—neither in the narrative mode, nor in the direct address mode. These lines enable a shift and highlight the longevity of pain, remorse, and horror that a soldier feels.

6. In lines 11–14, the speaker is viewing another soldier through the lens, "misty panes," of a gas mask and, perhaps, the phosphorescent glow of exploding gas, which creates the "thick green light," contributes to the illusion of a "green sea" in which the soldier is quite literally drowning.

7. Here Owen would seem to be foreshadowing the incapacitation of soldiers in general, but directly he is referring to the soldiers' fatigue robbing them of their attention to save themselves. They have lost the ability to see or hear the danger and the ability to flee it because they are so tired.

8. Owen likens the soldier's expression to "the devil's sick of sin," suggesting an oppression of soul from one who has seen the ultimate in egregious inhumanity. Responses will vary.

9. The reader should easily be swayed by the author's depiction of war that it is neither "sweet," nor "fitting to die" in such a manner as he describes.

10. Responses will vary.

Vocabulary

1. knock-kneed (2)—having knees that turn inward toward one another rather than straight up
2. writhing (19)—twisting and distorting
3. vile (24)—horrible

■ "The Bride Comes to Yellow Sky" by Stephen Crane—p. 668

Questions on Content, Structure, and Style

1. Some consider the West in Crane's stories as much of a character as the people he sketches. In this story, how does the setting in the opening scene set the mood for the story?
2. What main impressions do we have of the bride from descriptions of her?

3. Why is the passenger in paragraph 14 amused by the bride's "clumsy coquetry"?
4. What do the marshal's red hands signify initially? Is this same impression found later in the story?
5. A description of the coach the bride and groom ride in is recalled later in the story (paragraph 78). What does this coach signify to the bride and groom initially? When recalled later by Marshal Potter?
6. What is the purpose of the drummer character in this tale?
7. Which incidents reveal Scratchy Wilson's true character?
8. How does the relationship between Wilson and Potter clarify Potter's position in town?
9. Crane makes much ado of Potter's cowardice in not informing the citizens of Yellow Sky about his marriage. Can Potter be considered a coward? How or how not?
10. What does the bride come to represent in this tale of the Wild West?

Answers to Questions

1. The opening scene on the train suggests both westward movement and speed toward it. The "Pullman" reflects a luxurious form of transportation delivered from the east (and one from a bygone era). The descriptions of things seen out the windows reveal little to no industrial progress, save the train itself and the "sweeping into the east" of the little civilization that does exist. We are swept along toward a "precipice" or into an age and place about to change. Here the west is wild and yet untamed. Descriptions of the bride and groom, the porters, the behaviors of other passengers, all reflect a certain manner and decorum belonging to ages past and/or to differences in class. Feelings of discomfort and embarrassment stem from an understanding that the bride and groom are out of their usual element. The mood is tense and a bit mysterious and the cause is related to something in the west.

2. Her own appearance, "not pretty, nor was she very young" (3), easily embarrasses the bride. She is overweight and underclass (3). She likes to eat and isn't above saying so, obtusely anyway (14). She is incapable of dealing with the reality of the place her new husband is taking her to (75), and she is a self-focused woman who is grateful to be married and to a man of some importance, even if it is in a town far removed from civilization.

3. This passenger represents experience and the cynicism and scorn derived from viewing innocence corrupted by time and accident, or design. He represents the east and civilization.

4. Initially, the marshal's hands are a result of extensive time in the sun, alluding to the fact that he probably works outside. Ruddy hands and faces generally reveal a stereotypical common working class person. But the attention Crane gives to them suggests that perhaps they symbolize something more than sunburn or class. We might suspect that his hands represent those of a thief if we associate the idea to the term "caught red-handed." Because we know that the bride is not young, we can rule out chicanery in that sense. If the redness is equated to guilt, we might conclude that his hands symbolize his own condemnation of his actions. But in the end, we see that his duty to the town is of the highest order in that he is its defense against the wild behavior of Scratchy Wilson. So the initial impression of some sort of devious behavior is forgotten when we learn his real role. However, he is clearly domesticating his own life and, as we discover later, those of the residents in Yellow Sky, but without their permission, thus returning us to the question not of his cowardice but of his guilt.

5. The coach signifies opulence to the bride and groom as well as progress (4–9). It does not just transport people—it transports ideas. As railways became more prominent, more and more people moved west and its wildness was tamed, domesticated. Civilization of the American landscape shifted to accommodate more refined tastes and behaviors. Potter's recollection in paragraph 78 is recognition of his role in this usurpation of the "Wild West's" unwritten rules and accepted traditions of street fighting justice and independence.

6. The drummer serves as a vehicle for the story of the town's predicament. As an outsider, he is alarmed and fascinated by the rough behavior of Scratchy and the townspeople's resignation to it. But he is there to move the story along and has little other significance, except as another character of the "more civilized" east.

7. Scratchy purposely misses the dog when he shoots at it. We know he is an excellent shot from witnesses' accounts, so his missing the dog reveals both his desire for sport and his good heart. The same is true when he gives up "the game" after realizing Potter is married. He knows he's bested and needs to move west or give up his behavior. He could easily shoot the marshal, but much more enjoys the game they have been playing—one of besting, via gunfights. Here we understand the game as dangerous, but not ill intentioned, giving us a view of the west as fair, honest, and only a bit wicked.

8. The town's people rely on Potter to maintain the status quo. His courage allows them to be cowards. His breach of trust comes with his inability to tell them he is married. He can't tell them because he knows he is bringing change and domestication to the town. He sees this breach as the town's people will see it—that he can no longer support the status quo. The people will lose faith in his courage to protect them and understand, as does Scratchy Wilson, that they will soon have to reckon with the coming changes.

9. Ironically, Potter's position when he meets Scratchy in the street reveals his real courage—he has no gun and challenges the man to accept that he's unarmed and if Scratchy's "goin' to shoot [him] up, [he'd] better begin now" (80). There is also humor in the realization that Scratchy isn't out for blood, but that his little boy "shoot 'em up" days are gone. Paragraph 90 shows him shuffling off into the desert in his "sledding boys" boots, defeated by his enemy's marriage. It is Potter who has the courage to meet new challenges, like marriage, domestication, law—civilizing influences—while at the same time standing up to a drunken man with a gun while he, himself, has none.

10. The bride represents all manner of civilizing influences and progress, but with a twist. She who "had cooked and expected to cook, dutifully" (3) is out of her element in the train car, but her very being there and married reveals that she, like the train car is a vehicle of change and progress. She sees her low class as having been elevated through her marriage to an important man. It is debatable whether or not she has the ability to understand the effects her marriage will have on the town, but she trusts her husband to make it all right, because that is what is expected of her. In this regard she is an empty vessel, whose only substance is her own physical weight and her social standing. So as a civilizing influence, she is merely an accessory to the "crime."

Vocabulary

1. derisive (10)—mocking, scornful
2. coquetry (10)—an effort without true feeling to attract admiration
3. sardonic (14)—scornful and amused with it
4. plains-craft (21)—knowledge and skill in living on the plains

5. cadence (29)—rhythmic beat, of sound or activity
6. fatuously (30)—foolishly, without thought
7. bureau (33)— a dresser of drawers
8. Winchester (56)—a rifle
9. imperturbable (68)—unmoving, fixed in position or belief
10. lithely (68)—flexibly, resiliently
11. fusilladed (68)—being rapidly shot at
12. epithets (70)—abusive words or phrases attached or associated to a person or thing
13. apparitional (75)—ghost-like
14. galoots (82)—people who are odd or foolish

■ "A Jury of Her Peers" by Susan Glaspell—p. 675

Questions on Content, Structure, and Style

1. From what point of view is Glaspell writing?
2. What important details about Mrs. Hale do paragraphs two and nine reveal? Can you find other instances of a similar characterization?
3. Why does Mrs. Hale pull out Mrs. Wright's bad stitching and re-sew it in paragraph 167?
4. Is the setting in this story critical to our understanding? How?
5. What images are particularly strong? How do they help the reader comprehend the situation?
6. Which incidents are the most revealing to Mrs. Peter's character?
7. How do the men's repeated dismissals of the women's concerns contribute to the women's role in general? To their importance in solving the crime?
8. How is the dead bird connected to Mrs. Wright's guilt or innocence? Explain.
9. What assumptions to the men make about Mr. Wright's death and why?
10. What main theme(s) do you detect in this short story?

Answers to Questions

1. Primarily we view the story through the perceptions of Mrs. Hale with some internal monologue taking place. Mostly the story is in dialogue so that we have a limited perception based on what is said. Physical movement and exchanges are in the form of description from a limited narrator.
2. These two paragraphs reveal Mrs. Hale's feelings of guilt. There are many references to these feelings. Some are associated with herself and others with Mrs. Wright. See paragraphs 11, 21, 24, 26, 34, 82, 104, 107, 111, 116, 124, 142, 148, and 167.
3. Mrs. Hale pulls out the stitching partly because she believes the stitching is evidence of Mrs. Wright's guilt and partly because of her own guilt associated with not keeping up appearances, leaving things unfinished, untidy, etc. Guilty feelings Mrs. Hale has regarding not visiting Mrs. Wright contribute to her associating poor housekeeping and bad stitching to signs that Mrs. Wright was not in her right mind and, although she never states it, thus to Mrs. Wright's guilt in killing Mr. Wright.
4. The setting of a desolate farm on a winter prairie helps to set a mood of alienation or separateness. The farmhouse kitchen, ironically, brings the women together emotionally, bonds them in the association of like chores, responsibilities, struggles, positions, etc.

Where the ladies are unalike in position or child rearing, they share a common understanding of what it is like to be a wife on the prairie. The juxtaposition of isolation/coldness to connection/warmth contributes to our comprehension of why the women come to the conclusion they do, at least in part. It also helps to see that the men leave the kitchen more than once and don't give the kitchen much thought beyond a cursory notation that it is less than tidy.

5. Responses will vary. However, it should be noted that images of the two women together in paragraphs 10 and 12 suggest early on that they are bonded by feeling, even though they do not yet know it. A number of exchanges, both verbal and silent, continue to create a conspiracy of belief and, in the end, action.

6. Mrs. Peter's character is more difficult to decipher as most of the description comes from Mrs. Hale's point of view and is colored by her guilt. She feels distanced from Mrs. Peters for several reasons—she does not know her well, Mrs. Peters is married to the sheriff and thus holds some position, and she suspects that because she is married to the sheriff that she will be biased against Mrs. Wright. The narrator gives us several clues to Mrs. Peter's timidity, but in paragraph 243 we understand her strength in defense of justice.

7. The men regard women's concerns as trifling—too insignificant to concern the men. As such they overlook clues the women see. In this, the men contribute to the women's perceptions as well as their deductions and conspiracy to conceal their findings and thoughts.

8. The dead bird's wrung neck obviously echoes Mr. Wright's noosed one. The conclusions that are drawn from the bird involve placing blame on Mr. Wright for its death and thus his own. He snuffed the life out of Mrs. Wright over the years—according to Mrs. Hale's interpretation. So, in essence, he got what he deserved—justice, prairie-style, if you will. However, there is no actual evidence of how the bird died, or of Mrs. Wright strangling her husband. The women conjecture based on their own feelings of oppression and injustice.

9. The men, on the other hand, assume that Mrs. Wright must be the culprit because they can find no evidence to prove otherwise. But neither do they find evidence that she is guilty and, in fact, find it funny that the man could not fight a woman off. But they don't question this at all, assuming that Mrs. Wright's sheer proximity makes her the most likely suspect.

10. Students should see themes of gender differences, justice, revenge, and alienation, at least.

Vocabulary

1. queer (32)—odd, unusual
2. ungainly (68)—lacking in grace or refinement; clumsy
3. conceded (202)—agreed, to give value to another's opinion or position
4. petticoat (267)—an undergarment used by women as a slip or to fill out a skirt, usually with ruffles
5. incisively (271)—with exactness or precision

Chapter 34

Writers on Reading and Writing

p. 691

■ **"How Mr. Dewey Decimal Saved My Life"
by Barbara Kingsolver—p. 691**

Questions on Content, Structure, and Style

1. Kingsolver writes that "Miss Truman Richey snatched me from the jaws of ruin" (1). What does she mean by this?
2. What details does Kingsolver use to describe her existence? How are these details important to shaping her life?
3. What future does Kingsolver think Miss Richey saw for her? What do you think Miss Richey really saw?
4. How does the Dewey Decimal system play into the changes in Kingsolver's life?
5. Describe the tone of this essay. Point to strategies Kingsolver uses to reveal her tone.
6. What sorts of figurative language are used in paragraphs four through six? How does this language contribute to our understanding of Kingsolver's predicament?
7. In paragraph eleven, Kingsolver claims that "the walls of my high school dropped down and I caught the scent of the world." What does she mean by this? What is her reaction to it?
8. How was Kingsolver different from her classmates?

9. Do you think the author would have turned to writing as a profession if Miss Richey had not put her to work?

10. Can you think of any individuals in your life, other than family, who influenced you to see yourself in relation to the world in a different way?

Answers to Questions

1. Miss Richey enabled the author to see a future full of possibilities rather than the dim and dangerous ones she imagined she would have.

2. Kingsolver includes ideas about the fiscally poor educational system in Kentucky at the time, the diminished activity of a two-stop-light-town, pregnant classmates, suspended classmates, and general boredom. Having grown up with no or few examples of a future beyond what she sees in her own town, she is hard-pressed to imagine a future much different from those around her. As such her boredom becomes her motivation for escape.

3. Kingsolver thought Miss Richey saw her as a girl wanting to get into trouble with the local motorcycle gang, but Miss Richey may have seen her potential as a student. More likely though, she saw her as an assistant to help her organize the library.

4. The system forced the author to methodically address every text on the library's shelves. Proximity and cross-referencing forced her to look into the books themselves and one thing led to another as she found herself reading for enjoyment. Her reading thus opened her mind to her own potential and she began to understand the world in new ways.

5. The tone in the essay is both self-deprecating and feisty. The reader is at first led to believe that the narrator is a loser, but we see her potential as well, much in the way Miss Richey may have. She pretends to be surly and makes up "shocking, entirely untrue stories about . . . home life" (6). She imagines ruining her reputation for the pure thrill of it, but realizes she isn't the type of beauty that can pull it off (6). She uses sarcasm to define her values (8), and reveals her actions as at odds with what she thinks (10). In other words, she has created a character in crisis that works well for the story.

6. Some notable examples of figurative language include "like a reckless hiker gobbling up all the rations on day one of the long march" (4), "connected to my head by little cartoon bubbles" (5), "I clawed like a cat in a gunnysack against the doom I feared (6). These and others provide clear images of a bored, frustrated, and out-of-control teen.

7. Here Kingsolver's view of her future opens before her as she begins to "smell" her own potential as a writer. The thought of carving out a future beyond the confines of her town is intoxicating and she begins to develop a rich imagination that leads then to her own writing.

8. Kingsolver does not fit in with her classmates as she has an avid curiosity about the world to begin with. Thus she takes every class offered and runs out of options. She is not content to let the world shape her existence. Thus she is a prime candidate for growth through reading.

9. This author does, but answers may vary.

10. Responses will vary here as well and might be used as a prewriting opportunity for a longer paper. However, rather than having students write about the most influential person in their lives, a short story about an incident in their lives that began with an chance meeting and that reveals the details of how they, themselves, initiated a new path in their own lives might provide a more interesting and less hackneyed approach to this question.

Vocabulary

1. rationing (4)—saving, pacing one's assumptions
2. rations (4)—an allotment of food, generally, but also any items portioned out
3. interludes (4)—an entertaining space of time between other things
4. fathom (5)—a unit of depth measurement, or in this case, to comprehend or under-stand deeply
5. discerned (5)—distinguished something or someone from another or a background
6. surly (6)—a dark or rude attitude
7. myopic (6)—shortsighted or nearsighted/without discernment
8. tangible (10)—touchable
9. transcendent (11)—beyond experience

■ "Notes on Punctuation" by Lewis Thomas—p. 693

Questions on Content, Structure, and Style

1. What is the effect of the first parenthesis on the reader? The final 12?
2. What are the four stops Fowler claims English contains? Why do you think he says "the question mark and exclamation point are indicators of tone"? How does Thomas prove this point?
3. What does the author mean by "if the parentheses were left out with nothing to work with but the stops we would have considerably more flexibility in the deploying of layers of meaning" in paragraph 1?
4. What is Thomas' attitude toward his topic?
5. How does his own punctuation usage support or not support his points in paragraphs 3, 4, and 5?
6. Why does Thomas believe that an "exclamation point in a poem . . . is enough to destroy the whole work"?
7. To what does the author refer in the final paragraph when he writes "but you can't sit, not even take a breath, just because of a comma"? How does this statement reveal his thesis?

Answers to Questions

1. The first parenthesis should make the reader slow down. The second and successive parentheses may cause a reader to go back and reread or skip over them. The final 12 parentheses should also cause the reader to pause again, perhaps count them, and to reread the entire paragraph. The effect will depend on the reader.
2. Fowler claims the four stops to be the comma, the semicolon, the colon, and the period. The question mark forces the reader's voice, internal or verbalized, to rise and the exclamation point forces the reader's voice into either a shout or stronger emphasis at the very least. Thomas proves this point by contrasting the question mark with the semicolon as used by the Greeks in the example of "Why weepest thou"(1).
3. Having students rewrite this sentence without the parentheses will reveal the many options for altered meaning through use of other types of punctuation.
4. Thomas's attitude might best be described as playful.

5. In paragraph 3, Thomas discusses the expectation for the reader that the semicolon produces, that something more will follow; he uses it excessively to illustrate his point. The same is true in paragraph 4 wherein he describes the colon as preceding a series of things: a list, a set of points, a numbering or ordering of ideas. Here he ends the paragraph, however, with a contrasting focus on commas used with present participles that allow the reader to follow the points being made without feeling as though being directed. In paragraph 5, he discusses the exclamation point and again uses it in the context that best exemplifies his meaning, which is that they often attract attention unnecessarily!

6. Students' responses will vary. They should note that Thomas is working within an aesthetic that favors finesse, syntactical precision, and subtlety in poetry. Moreover, ambiguity, which he claims the exclamation point and the question mark would bring to a poem, is the one element of poetry that causes us to read closely, so that when meaning is derived it comes from the reader joining in the making of it with the writer. Being shouted at or directed to question a thought or an image may create the kind of ambiguity the poet won't want—the feeling a reader would most certainly have toward the poem.

7. Every student should recognize the elementary school maxim to "Place a comma where you would take a breath." Thomas ends with commas. He also begins his discussion of Fowler's "stops" with commas and then proceeds through a discussion of the effects of major punctuation marks. His strategy here is to define boundaries of punctuation usage through contexts of purpose and voice and meaning, rather than rules. Rules should be the last reason the writer considers using punctuation, unless one is writing *about* them.

Vocabulary

1. deploying (1)—placing or arranging for future use
2. exactitude (1)—the quality of being precise
3. ambiguity (1)—the condition of having more than one meaning understood
4. minnows (1)—small, insignificant fish often used as bait
5. banal (5)—common, lacking originality
6. parsimonious (8)—stingy, overly frugal or thrifty

■ "Mother Tongue" by Amy Tan—p. 695

Questions on Content, Structure, and Style

1. One of Tan's purposes in this essay could be regarded as a search for her authentic voice. Do you think she finds it? If so, how does she define it?

2. Tan's discussion of speaking several Englishes might be recognizable to you if you've grown up speaking more than one language or using mixed languages such as Spanglish. Can you relate to her struggle in other ways that may be more universal?

3. Who is Tan's audience? How can you tell?

4. How would you categorize this essay—narrative, process analysis, argument, something other?

5. What contributing factors led to Tan's desire to write this essay? What was her primary reason?

6. What does Tan note in paragraph 2 that influenced her to be a writer?

7. Speculate on influences other than those noted in paragraph 2 that may have caused her to become a writer.

8. How does paragraph 17 contribute to your understanding of why she chose to write rather than enter a profession in a math-related field, as she was encouraged to do?

9. While linguists might describe language in terms of sound, pronunciation, order, and meaning and grammarians in terms of rules and usage, how does language function for Tan? What does she examine?

10. In paragraph 20, Tan relates a line of text she omitted from her novel *The Joy Luck Club*. Why did she choose to omit it?

Answers to Questions

1. She finds it in her mother's speech, which she claims as her own when she names it as her mother tongue—the one she knows intimately and unconsciously, but becomes aware of only when she reflects on her mother's response to her book. She defines it as "vivid, direct, full of observation, and imagery"(7).

2. Students should be able to relate in terms of dialects they use with their friends versus those used at work or in the home or even with strangers. They may want to discuss how speech patterns differ and what patterns impart to the listener about self.

3. Tan is writing to those who have asked her questions about her writing, but her reflection is learned, even though she declares it mere opinion. It is considered and thoughtful and speaks to issues of language and language learning, so that she is most likely addressing both writers and students of writing as well as her colleagues and those curious about her as a curiosity—a successful Asian-American writer (18).

4. While Tan uses narrative techniques to relay her message, she is focused on showing cause and effect.

5. Being asked to give a speech about her writing (3), having her mother in the audience and realizing she was using a kind of English she had never used with her mother (3), realizing that speech with her mother is habitual, familiar, and unnoticed as such on a day-to-day basis (4), understanding that people wrongly believe that those who speak imperfectly are somehow "broken" or less intellectually capable (7, 8), discovering the serious consequences or effects of such misperceptions when her mother could not get needed information from medical personnel (14), her own struggles with writing and tests in school (15–17), and finally because she was asked "why there are not more Asian Americans represented in American Literature. Why are there few Asian Americans enrolled in creative writing programs? Why do so many Chinese students go into engineering?" all contribute to her desire to write this essay. The latter set of questions would seem to be her primary reason for writing, so that this essay becomes her examination of causes and effect in an attempt to answer those questions.

6. She loves language, is "fascinated by language in daily life," spends time thinking about its "power" to "evoke an emotion, a visual image, a complex idea, or a simple truth" (2).

7. Responses will vary, but a primary influence most certainly must have been the fact that she spent most of her young life speaking for her mother, translating meaning for others, using a variety of Englishes in order to make meaning.